THE PELICAN SHAKESPEARE
GENERAL EDITORS

STEPHEN ORGEL
A. R. BRAUNMULLER

Pericles
Prince of Tyre

The resuscitation of Thaisa (III.2). Frontispiece to the play in
Nicholas Rowe's Shakespeare, 1709, the first illustrated edition.
The play was in the repertory of Davenant's company after the
Restoration, but by 1709 it had not been performed for half
a century, and the thoroughly classicized decor probably
does not reflect stage practice.

William Shakespeare

—

Pericles
Prince of Tyre

EDITED BY STEPHEN ORGEL

PENGUIN BOOKS

PENGUIN BOOKS
An imprint of Penguin Random House LLC
penguinrandomhouse.com

Pericles Prince of Tyre edited by James G. McManaway published in
Penguin Books (USA) 1967
Revised edition published 1977
Edition edited by Stephen Orgel published 2001
This edition published 2019

LIBRARY OF CONGRESS CATALOGING-IN-PUBLICATION DATA
Shakespeare, William, 1564–1616.
Pericles Prince of Tyre / William Shakespeare ; edited by Stephen Orgel.
p.   cm. (The Pelican Shakespeare)
ISBN 978-0-14-071469-2 (pbk.)
1. Princes—Lebanon—Tyre—Drama.
I. Orgel, Stephen. II. Title. III. Series.
PR2830.A2 074 2001
822.3'3—dc21   2001031339

Printed in the United States of America
Set in Adobe Garamond
Designed by Virginia Norey

Contents

Publisher's Note   vii

The Theatrical World   ix

The Texts of Shakespeare   xxv

Introduction   xxxi

Note on the Text   xlvii

Pericles Prince of Tyre   1

Publisher's Note

THE PELICAN SHAKESPEARE has served generations of readers as an authoritative series of texts and scholarship since the first volume appeared under the general editorship of Alfred Harbage over half a century ago. In the past decades, new editions followed to reflect the profound changes textual and critical studies of Shakespeare have undergone. The texts of the plays and poems were thoroughly revised in accordance with leading scholarship, and in some cases were entirely reedited. New introductions and notes were provided in all the volumes. The Pelican Shakespeare was designed as a successor to the original series; the previous editions had been taken into account, and the advice of the previous editors was solicited where it was feasible to do so. The current editions include updated bibliographic references to recent scholarship.

Certain textual features of the new Pelican Shakespeare should be particularly noted. All lines are numbered that contain a word, phrase, or allusion explained in the glossarial notes. In addition, for convenience, every tenth line is also numbered, in italics when no annotation is indicated. The intrusive and often inaccurate place headings inserted by early editors are omitted (as has become standard practice), but for the convenience of those who miss them, an indication of locale now appears as the first item in the annotation of each scene.

In the interest of both elegance and utility, each speech prefix is set in a separate line when the speakers' lines are in verse, except when those words form the second half of a verse line. Thus the verse form of the speech is kept visually intact. What is printed as verse and what is printed as prose has, in general, the authority of the original texts. Departures from the original texts in this regard have the authority only of editorial tradition and the judgment of the Pelican editors; and, in a few instances, are admittedly arbitrary.

The Theatrical World

Economic REALITIES determined the theatrical world in which Shakespeare's plays were written, performed, and received. For centuries in England, the primary theatrical tradition was nonprofessional. Craft guilds (or "mysteries") provided religious drama – mystery plays – as part of the celebration of religious and civic festivals, and schools and universities staged classical and neoclassical drama in both Latin and English as part of their curricula. In these forms, drama was established and socially acceptable. Professional theater, in contrast, existed on the margins of society. The acting companies were itinerant; playhouses could be any available space – the great halls of the aristocracy, town squares, civic halls, inn yards, fair booths, or open fields – and income was sporadic, dependent on the passing of the hat or on the bounty of local patrons. The actors, moreover, were considered little better than vagabonds, constantly in danger of arrest or expulsion.

In the late 1560s and 1570s, however, English professional theater began to gain respectability. Wealthy aristocrats fond of drama – the Lord Admiral, for example, or the Lord Chamberlain – took acting companies under their protection so that the players technically became members of their households and were no longer subject to arrest as homeless or masterless men. Permanent theaters were first built at this time as well, allowing the companies to control and charge for entry to their performances.

Shakespeare's livelihood, and the stunning artistic explosion in which he participated, depended on pragmatic and architectural effort. Professional theater requires ways to restrict access to its offerings; if it does not, and admission fees cannot be charged, the actors do not get paid, the costumes go to a pawnbroker, and there is no such thing as a professional, ongoing theatrical tradition. The answer to that economic need arrived in the late 1560s and 1570s with the creation of the so-called public or amphitheater playhouse. Recent discoveries indicate that the precursor of the Globe playhouse in London (where Shakespeare's mature plays were presented) and the Rose theater (which presented Christopher Marlowe's plays and some of Shakespeare's earliest ones) was the Red Lion theater of 1567. Archaeological studies of the foundations of the Rose and Globe theaters have revealed that the open-air theater of the 1590s and later was probably a polygonal building with fourteen to twenty or twenty-four sides, multistoried, from 75 to 100 feet in diameter, with a raised, partly covered "thrust" stage that projected into a group of standing patrons, or "groundlings," and a covered gallery, seating up to 2,500 or more (very crowded) spectators.

These theaters might have been about half full on any given day, though the audiences were larger on holidays or when a play was advertised, as old and new were, through printed playbills posted around London. The metropolitan area's late-Tudor, early-Stuart population (circa 1590–1620) has been estimated at about 150,000 to 250,000. It has been supposed that in the mid-1590s there were about 15,000 spectators per week at the public theaters; thus, as many as 10 percent of the local population went to the theater regularly. Consequently, the theaters' repertories – the plays available for this experienced and frequent audience – had to change often: in the month between September 15 and October 15, 1595, for instance, the Lord Admiral's Men performed twenty-eight times in eighteen different plays.

Since natural light illuminated the amphitheaters' stages, performances began between noon and two o'clock and ran without a break for two or three hours. They often concluded with a jig, a fencing display, or some other nondramatic exhibition. Weather conditions determined the season for the amphitheaters: plays were performed every day (including Sundays, sometimes, to clerical dismay) except during Lent – the forty days before Easter – or periods of plague, or sometimes during the summer months when law courts were not in session and the most affluent members of the audience were not in London.

To a modern theatergoer, an amphitheater stage like that of the Rose or Globe would appear an unfamiliar mixture of plainness and elaborate decoration. Much of the structure was carved or painted, sometimes to imitate marble; elsewhere, as under the canopy projecting over the stage, to represent the stars and the zodiac. Appropriate painted canvas pictures (of Jerusalem, for example, if the play was set in that city) were apparently hung on the wall behind the acting area, and tragedies were accompanied by black hangings, presumably something like crepe festoons or bunting. Although these theaters did not employ what we would call scenery, early modern spectators saw numerous large props, such as the "bar" at which a prisoner stood during a trial, the "mossy bank" where lovers reclined, an arbor for amorous conversation, a chariot, gallows, tables, trees, beds, thrones, writing desks, and so forth. Audiences might learn a scene's location from a sign (reading "Athens," for example) carried across the stage (as in Bertolt Brecht's twentieth-century productions). Equally captivating (and equally irritating to the theater's enemies) were the rich costumes and personal props the actors used: the most valuable items in the surviving theatrical inventories are the swords, gowns, robes, crowns, and other items worn or carried by the performers.

Magic appealed to Shakespeare's audiences as much as it does to us today, and the theater exploited many deceptive and spectacular devices. A winch in the loft above the stage, called "the heavens," could lower and raise actors playing gods, goddesses, and other supernatural figures to and from the main acting area, just as one or more trapdoors permitted entrances and exits to and from the area, called "hell," beneath the stage. Actors wore elementary makeup such as wigs, false beards, and face paint, and they employed pigs' bladders filled with animal blood to make wounds seem more real. They had rudimentary but effective ways of pretending to behead or hang a person. Supernumeraries (stagehands or actors not needed in a particular scene) could make thunder sounds (by shaking a metal sheet or rolling an iron ball down a chute) and show lightning (by blowing inflammable resin through tubes into a flame). Elaborate fireworks enhanced the effects of dragons flying through the air or imitated such celestial phenomena as comets, shooting stars, and multiple suns. Horses' hoofbeats, bells (located perhaps in the tower above the stage), trumpets and drums, clocks, cannon shots and gunshots, and the like were common sound effects. And the music of viols, cornets, oboes, and recorders was a regular feature of theatrical performances.

For two relatively brief spans, from the late 1570s to 1590 and from 1599 to 1614, the amphitheaters competed with the so-called private, or indoor, theaters, which originated as, or later represented themselves as, educational institutions training boys as singers for church services and court performances. These indoor theaters had two features that were distinct from the amphitheaters': their personnel and their playing spaces. The amphitheaters' adult companies included both adult men, who played the male roles, and boys, who played the female roles; the private, or indoor, theater companies, on the other hand, were entirely composed of boys aged about 8 to 16, who were, or could pretend to be, candidates for singers in a church or a royal boys' choir. (Until 1660, professional theatrical companies included no women.) The playing space would appear much more familiar to modern audiences than the long-vanished amphitheaters; the later indoor theaters were, in fact, the ancestors of the typical modern theater. They were enclosed spaces, usually rectangular, with the stage filling one end of the rectangle and the audience arrayed in seats or benches across (and sometimes lining) the building's longer axis. These spaces staged plays less frequently than the public theaters (perhaps only once a week) and held far fewer spectators than the amphitheaters: about 200 to 600, as opposed to 2,500 or more. Fewer patrons mean a smaller gross income, unless each pays more. Not surprisingly, then, private theaters charged higher prices than the amphitheaters, probably sixpence, as opposed to a penny for the cheapest entry.

Protected from the weather, the indoor theaters presented plays later in the day than the amphitheaters, and used artificial illumination – candles in sconces or candelabra. But candles melt, and need replacing, snuffing, and trimming, and these practical requirements may have been part of the reason the indoor theaters introduced breaks in the performance, the intermission so dear to the heart of theatergoers and to the pocketbooks of theater concessionaires ever since. Whether motivated by the need to tend to the candles or by the entrepreneurs' wishing to sell oranges and liquor, or both, the indoor theaters eventually established the modern convention of the non-continuous performance. In the early modern "private" theater, musical performances apparently filled the intermissions, which in Stuart theater jargon seem to have been called "acts."

At the end of the first decade of the seventeenth century, the distinction between public amphitheaters and private indoor companies ceased. For various cultural, political, and economic reasons, individual companies gained control of both the public, open-air theaters and the indoor ones, and companies mixing adult men and boys took over the formerly "private" theaters. Despite the death of the boys' companies and of their highly innova-

tive theaters (for which such luminous playwrights as
Ben Jonson, George Chapman, and John Marston wrote),
their playing spaces and conventions had an immense impact on subsequent plays: not merely for the intervals
(which stressed the artistic and architectonic importance
of "acts"), but also because they introduced political and
social satire as a popular dramatic ingredient, even in
tragedy, and a wider range of actorly effects, encouraged
by their more intimate playing spaces.

Even the briefest sketch of the Shakespearean theatrical
world would be incomplete without some comment on
the social and cultural dimensions of theaters and playing
in the period. In an intensely hierarchical and status-
conscious society, professional actors and their ventures had
hardly any respectability; as we have indicated, to protect
themselves against laws designed to curb vagabondage and
the increase of masterless men, actors resorted to the near-
fiction that they were the servants of noble masters, and
wore their distinctive livery. Hence the company for which
Shakespeare wrote in the 1590s that called itself the Lord
Chamberlain's Men and pretended that the public, money-
getting performances were in fact rehearsals for private performances before that high court official. From 1598, the
Privy Council had licensed theatrical companies, and after
1603, with the accession of King James I, the companies
gained explicit royal protection, just as the Queen's Men
had for a time under Queen Elizabeth. The Chamberlain's
Men became the King's Men, and the other companies
were patronized by the other members of the royal family.

These designations were legal fictions that half-
concealed an important economic and social development, the evolution away from the theater's organization
on the model of the guild, a self-regulating confraternity
of individual artisans, into a proto-capitalist organization.
Shakespeare's company became a joint-stock company,
where persons who supplied capital and, in some cases,

such as Shakespeare's, capital and talent, employed themselves and others in earning a return on that capital. This development meant that actors and theater companies were outside both the traditional guild structures, which required some form of civic or royal charter, and the feudal household organization of master-and-servant. This anomalous, maverick social and economic condition made theater companies practically unruly and potentially even dangerous; consequently, numerous official bodies – including the London metropolitan and ecclesiastical authorities as well as, occasionally, the royal court itself – tried, without much success, to control and even to disband them.

Public officials had good reason to want to close the theaters: they were attractive nuisances – they drew often riotous crowds, they were always noisy, and they could be politically offensive and socially insubordinate. Until the Civil War, however, anti-theatrical forces failed to shut down professional theater, for many reasons – limited surveillance and few police powers, tensions or outright hostilities among the agencies that sought to check or channel theatrical activity, and lack of clear policies for control. Another reason must have been the theaters' undeniable popularity. Curtailing any activity enjoyed by such a substantial percentage of the population was difficult, as various Roman emperors attempting to limit circuses had learned, and the Tudor-Stuart audience was not merely large, it was socially diverse and included women. The prevalence of public entertainment in this period has been underestimated. In fact, fairs, holidays, games, sporting events, the equivalent of modern parades, freak shows, and street exhibitions all abounded, but the theater was the most widely and frequently available entertainment to which people of every class had access. That fact helps account both for its quantity and for the fear and anger it aroused.

Books About Shakespeare's Theater

Useful scholarly studies of theatrical life in Shakespeare's day include: G. E. Bentley, *The Jacobean and Caroline Stage*, 7 vols. (1941–68), and the same author's *The Professions of Dramatist and Player in Shakespeare's Time, 1590–1642* (1986); Julian Bowsher, *The Rose Theatre: An Archaeological Discovery* (1998); E. K. Chambers, *The Elizabethan Stage*, 4 vols. (1923); Christine Eccles, *The Rose Theatre* (1990); R. A. Foakes, *Illustrations of the English Stage, 1580–1642* (1985); Andrew Gurr, *The Shakespearean Stage, 1574–1642*, 3rd ed. (1992), and the same author's *Playgoing in Shakespeare's London*, 2nd ed. (1996); Roslyn Lander Knutson, *Playing Companies and Commerce in Shakespeare's Time* (2001); Edwin Nungezer, *A Dictionary of Actors* (1929); Carol Chillington Rutter, ed., *Documents of the Rose Playhouse* (1984); Tiffany Stern, *Documents of Performance in Early Modern England* (2009); Glynne Wickham, Herbert Berry, and William Ingram, *English Professional Theatre, 1530–1660* (2009).

WILLIAM SHAKESPEARE OF
STRATFORD-UPON-AVON, GENTLEMAN

Many people have said that we know very little about William Shakespeare's life – pinheads and postcards are often mentioned as appropriately tiny surfaces on which to record the available information. More imaginatively and perhaps more correctly, Ralph Waldo Emerson wrote, "Shakespeare is the only biographer of Shakespeare. . . . So far from Shakespeare's being the least known, he is the one person in all modern history fully known to us."

In fact, we know more about Shakespeare's life than we do about almost any other English writer's of his era. His last will and testament (dated March 25, 1616) survives, as do numerous legal contracts and court documents involving Shakespeare as principal or witness, and parish records in Stratford and London. Shakespeare appears quite often in official records of King James's royal court, and of course Shakespeare's name appears on numerous title pages and in the written and recorded words of his literary contemporaries Robert Greene, Henry Chettle, Francis Meres, John Davies of Hereford, Ben Jonson, and many others. Indeed, if we make due allowance for the bloating of modern, run-of-the-mill bureaucratic records, more information has survived over the past four hundred years about William Shakespeare of Stratford-upon-Avon, Warwickshire, than is likely to survive in the next four hundred years about any reader of these words.

What we do not have are entire categories of information – Shakespeare's private letters or diaries, drafts and revisions of poems and plays, critical prefaces or essays, commendatory verse for other writers' works, or instructions guiding his fellow actors in their performances, for instance – that we imagine would help us understand and appreciate his surviving writings. For all we know, many such data never existed as written records. Many literary and theatrical critics, not knowing what might once have existed, more or less cheerfully accept the situation; some even make a theoretical virtue of it by claiming that such data are irrelevant to understanding and interpreting the plays and poems.

So, what do we know about William Shakespeare, the man responsible for thirty-seven or perhaps more plays, more than 150 sonnets, two lengthy narrative poems, and some shorter poems?

While many families by the name of Shakespeare (or some variant spelling) can be identified in the English Midlands as far back as the twelfth century, it seems likely that the dramatist's grandfather, Richard, moved to Snitterfield, a town not far from Stratford-upon-Avon, sometime before 1529. In Snitterfield, Richard Shakespeare leased farmland from the very wealthy Robert Arden. By 1552, Richard's son John had moved to a large house on

Henley Street in Stratford-upon-Avon, the house that
stands today as "The Birthplace." In Stratford, John
Shakespeare traded as a glover, dealt in wool, and lent
money at interest; he also served in a variety of civic posts,
including "High Bailiff," the municipality's equivalent of
mayor. In 1557, he married Robert Arden's youngest
daughter, Mary. Mary and John had four sons – William
was the oldest – and four daughters, of whom only Joan
outlived her most celebrated sibling. William was baptized
(an event entered in the Stratford parish church records)
on April 26, 1564, and it has become customary, without
any good factual support, to suppose he was born on April
23, which happens to be the feast day of Saint George, patron saint of England, and is also the date on which he
died, in 1616. Shakespeare married Anne Hathaway in
1582, when he was eighteen and she was twenty-six; their
first child was born five months later. It has been generally
assumed that the marriage was enforced and subsequently
unhappy, but these are only assumptions; it has been estimated, for instance, that up to one third of Elizabethan
brides were pregnant when they married. Anne and
William Shakespeare had three children: Susanna, who
married a prominent local physician, John Hall; and the
twins Hamnet, who died young in 1596, and Judith, who
married Thomas Quiney – apparently a rather shady individual. The name Hamnet was unusual but not unique: he
and his twin sister were named for their godparents,
Shakespeare's neighbors Hamnet and Judith Sadler. Shakespeare's father died in 1601 (the year of *Hamlet*), and Mary
Arden Shakespeare died in 1608 (the year of *Coriolanus*).
William Shakespeare's last surviving direct descendant was
his granddaughter Elizabeth Hall, who died in 1670.

    Between the birth of the twins in 1585 and a clear refer-
ence to Shakespeare as a practicing London dramatist in
Robert Greene's sensationalizing, satiric pamphlet, *Greene's
Groatsworth of Wit* (1592), there is no record of where
William Shakespeare was or what he was doing. These

seven so-called lost years have been imaginatively filled by scholars and other students of Shakespeare: some think he traveled to Italy, or fought in the Low Countries, or studied law or medicine, or worked as an apprentice actor/writer, and so on to even more fanciful possibilities. Whatever the biographical facts for those "lost" years, Greene's nasty remarks in 1592 testify to professional envy and to the fact that Shakespeare already had a successful career in London. Speaking to his fellow playwrights, Greene warns both generally and specifically:

> ... trust them [actors] not: for there is an upstart crow, beautified with our feathers, that with his tiger's heart wrapped in a player's hide supposes he is as well able to bombast out a blank verse as the best of you; and being an absolute Johannes Factotum, is in his own conceit the only Shake-scene in a country.

The passage mimics a line from *3 Henry VI* (hence the play must have been performed before Greene wrote) and seems to say that "Shake-scene" is both actor and playwright, a jack-of-all-trades. That same year, Henry Chettle protested Greene's remarks in *Kind-Heart's Dream,* and each of the next two years saw the publication of poems – *Venus and Adonis* and *The Rape of Lucrece,* respectively – publicly ascribed to (and dedicated by) Shakespeare. Early in 1595 he was named one of the senior members of a prominent acting company, the Lord Chamberlain's Men, when they received payment for court performances during the 1594 Christmas season.

Clearly, Shakespeare had achieved both success and reputation in London. In 1596, upon Shakespeare's application, the College of Arms granted his father the now-familiar coat of arms he had taken the first steps to obtain almost twenty years before, and in 1598, John's son – now permitted to call himself "gentleman" – took a 10 percent share in the new Globe playhouse. In 1597, he

bought a substantial bourgeois house, called New Place, in
Stratford – the garden remains, but Shakespeare's house,
several times rebuilt, was torn down in 1759 – and over
the next few years Shakespeare spent large sums buying
land and making other investments in the town and its
environs. Though he worked in London, his family remained in Stratford, and he seems always to have considered Stratford the home he would eventually return to.
Something approaching a disinterested appreciation of
Shakespeare's popular and professional status appears in
Francis Meres's *Palladis Tamia* (1598), a not especially
imaginative and perhaps therefore persuasive record of literary reputations. Reviewing contemporary English writers, Meres lists the titles of many of Shakespeare's plays,
including one not now known, *Love's Labor's Won,* and
praises his "mellifluous & hony-tongued" "sugred Sonnets," which were then circulating in manuscript (they
were first collected in 1609). Meres describes Shakespeare
as "one of the best" English playwrights of both comedy
and tragedy. In *Remains . . . Concerning Britain* (1605),
William Camden – a more authoritative source than the
imitative Meres – calls Shakespeare one of the "most
pregnant witts of these our times" and joins him with
such writers as Chapman, Daniel, Jonson, Marston, and
Spenser. During the first decades of the seventeenth century, publishers began to attribute numerous play quartos,
including some non-Shakespearean ones, to Shakespeare,
either by name or initials, and we may assume that they
deemed Shakespeare's name and supposed authorship,
true or false, commercially attractive.

For the next ten years or so, various records show
Shakespeare's dual career as playwright and man of the
theater in London, and as an important local figure in
Stratford. In 1608-9 his acting company – designated
the "King's Men" soon after King James had succeeded
Queen Elizabeth in 1603 – rented, refurbished, and
opened a small interior playing space, the Blackfriars the-

ater, in London, and Shakespeare was once again listed as a substantial sharer in the group of proprietors of the playhouse. By May 11, 1612, however, he describes himself as a Stratford resident in a London lawsuit – an indication that he had withdrawn from day-to-day professional activity and returned to the town where he had always had his main financial interests. When Shakespeare bought a substantial residential building in London, the Blackfriars Gatehouse, close to the theater of the same name, on March 10, 1613, he is recorded as William Shakespeare "of Stratford upon Avon in the county of Warwick, gentleman," and he named several London residents as the building's trustees. Still, he continued to participate in theatrical activity: when the new Earl of Rutland needed an allegorical design to bear as a shield, or *impresa,* at the celebration of King James's Accession Day, March 24, 1613, the earl's accountant recorded a payment of 44 shillings to Shakespeare for the device with its motto.

For the last few years of his life, Shakespeare evidently concentrated his activities in the town of his birth. Most of the final records concern business transactions in Stratford, ending with the notation of his death on April 23, 1616, and burial in Holy Trinity Church, Stratford-upon-Avon.

THE QUESTION OF AUTHORSHIP

The history of ascribing Shakespeare's plays (the poems do not come up so often) to someone else began, as it continues, peculiarly. The earliest published claim that someone else wrote Shakespeare's plays appeared in an 1856 article by Delia Bacon in the American journal *Putnam's Monthly* – although an Englishman, Thomas Wilmot, had shared his doubts in private (even secretive) conversations with friends near the end of the eighteenth century. Bacon's was a sad personal history that ended in madness and poverty, but the year after her article, she published, with great difficulty and the bemused assistance of Nathaniel Hawthorne (then United States Consul in Liverpool, England), her *Philosophy of the Plays of Shakspere Unfolded.* This huge, ornately written, confusing farrago is almost unreadable; sometimes its intents, to say nothing of its arguments, disappear entirely beneath near-raving, ecstatic writing. Tumbled in with much supposed "philosophy" appear the claims that Francis Bacon (from whom Delia Bacon eventually claimed descent), Walter Raleigh, and several other contemporaries of Shakespeare's had written the plays. The book had little impact except as a ridiculed curiosity.

Once proposed, however, the issue gained momentum among people whose conviction was the greater in proportion to their ignorance of sixteenth- and seventeenth-century English literature, history, and society. Another American amateur, Catharine F. Ashmead Windle, made the next influential contribution to the cause when she published *Report to the British Museum* (1882), wherein she promised to open "the Cipher of Francis Bacon," though what she mostly offers, in the words of S. Schoenbaum, is "demented allegorizing." An entire new cottage industry grew from Windle's suggestion that the texts contain hidden, cryptographically discoverable ciphers – "clues" – to their authorship; and today there are not only books devoted to the putative ciphers, but also pamphlets, journals, and newsletters.

Although Baconians have led the pack of those seeking a substitute Shakespeare, in *"Shakespeare" Identified* (1920), J. Thomas Looney became the first published "Oxfordian" when he proposed Edward de Vere, seventeenth earl of Oxford, as the secret author of Shakespeare's plays. Also for Oxford and his "authorship" there are today dedicated societies, articles, journals, and books. Less popular candidates – Queen Elizabeth and Christopher Marlowe among them – have had adherents, but the movement seems to have divided into two main contending factions, Baconian and Oxfordian. (For further details on all the candidates for "Shakespeare," see S. Schoenbaum, *Shakespeare's Lives,* 2nd ed., 1991.)

The Baconians, the Oxfordians, and supporters of other candidates have one trait in common – they are snobs. Every pro-Bacon or pro-Oxford tract sooner or later claims that the historical William Shakespeare of Stratford-upon-Avon could not have written the plays because he could not have had the training, the university education, the experience, and indeed the imagination or background their author supposedly possessed. Only a learned genius like Bacon or an aristocrat like Oxford could have written such fine plays. (As it happens, lucky male children of the middle class had access to better education than most aristocrats in Elizabethan England – and Oxford was not particularly well educated.) Shakespeare received in the Stratford grammar school a formal education that would daunt many college graduates today; and popular rival playwrights such as the very learned Ben Jonson and George Chapman, both of whom also lacked university training, achieved great artistic success, without being taken as Bacon or Oxford.

Besides snobbery, one other quality characterizes the authorship controversy: lack of evidence. A great deal of testimony from Shakespeare's time shows that Shakespeare wrote Shakespeare's plays and that his contemporaries recognized them as distinctive and distinctly superior. (Some of that contemporary evidence is collected in E. K. Chambers, *William Shakespeare: A Study of Facts and Problems,* 2 vols., 1930.) Since that testimony comes from Shakespeare's enemies and theatrical competitors as well as from his co-workers and from the Elizabethan equivalent of literary journalists, it seems unlikely that, if any of these sources had known he was a fraud, they would have failed to record that fact.

Books About Shakespeare's Life

The following books provide scholarly, documented accounts of Shakespeare's life: G. E. Bentley, *Shakespeare: A Biographical Handbook* (1961); E. K. Chambers, *William Shakespeare: A Study of Facts and Problems*, 2 vols. (1930); S. Schoenbaum, *William Shakespeare: A Compact Documentary Life* (1977), and the same author's *Shakespeare's Lives*, 2nd ed. (1991); James Shapiro, *Contested Will: Who Wrote Shakespeare?* (2010). Many scholarly editions of Shakespeare's complete works print brief compilations of essential dates and events. References to Shakespeare's works up to 1700 are collected in C. M. Ingleby et al., *Shakespeare Allusion-Book*, rev. ed., 2 vols. (1932).

The Texts of Shakespeare

AS FAR AS WE KNOW, only one manuscript conceivably in Shakespeare's own hand may (and even this is much disputed) exist: a few pages of a play called *Sir Thomas More,* which apparently was never performed. What we do have, as later readers, performers, scholars, students, are printed texts. The earliest of these survive in two forms: quartos and folios. Quartos (from the Latin for "four") are small books, printed on sheets of paper that were then folded twice, to make four leaves or eight pages. When these were bound together, the result was a squarish, eminently portable volume that sold for the relatively small sum of sixpence (translating in modern terms to about $5). In folios, on the other hand, the sheets are folded only once, in half, producing large, impressive volumes taller than they are wide. This was the format for important works of philosophy, science, theology, and literature (the major precedent for a folio Shakespeare was Ben Jonson's *Works,* 1616). The decision to print the works of a popular playwright in folio is an indication of how far up on the social scale the theatrical profession had come during Shakespeare's lifetime. The Shakespeare folio was an expensive book, selling for between fifteen and eighteen shillings, depending on the binding (in modern terms, from about $150 to $180). Twenty Shakespeare plays of the thirty-seven that survive first appeared in quarto, seventeen of which appeared during Shakespeare's lifetime; the rest of the plays are found only in folio.

The First Folio was published in 1623, seven years after Shakespeare's death, and was authorized by his fellow actors, the co-owners of the King's Men. This publication was certainly a mark of the company's enormous respect for Shakespeare; but it was also a way of turning the old plays, most of which were no longer current in the playhouse, into ready money (the folio includes only Shakespeare's plays, not his sonnets or other nondramatic verse). Whatever the motives behind the publication of the folio, the texts it preserves constitute the basis for almost all later editions of the playwright's works. The texts, however, differ from those of the earlier quartos, sometimes in minor respects but often significantly – most strikingly in the two texts of *King Lear*, but also in important ways in *Hamlet*, *Othello*, and *Troilus and Cressida*. (The variants are recorded in the textual notes to each play in the new Pelican series.) The differences in these texts represent, in a sense, the essence of theater: the texts of plays were initially not intended for publication. They were scripts, designed for the actors to perform – the principal life of the play at this period was in performance. And it follows that in Shakespeare's theater the playwright typically had no say either in how his play was performed or in the disposition of his text – he was an employee of the company. The authoritative figures in the theatrical enterprise were the shareholders in the company, who were for the most part the major actors. They decided what plays were to be done; they hired the playwright and often gave him an outline of the play they wanted him to write. Often, too, the play was a collaboration: the company would retain a group of writers, and parcel out the scenes among them. The resulting script was then the property of the company, and the actors would revise it as they saw fit during the course of putting it on stage. The resulting text belonged to the company. The playwright had no rights in it once he had been paid. (This system survives largely intact in the movie industry, and most of the playwrights of Shakespeare's time were as anonymous as most screenwriters are today.) The script could also, of course, continue to change as the tastes of audiences and the requirements of the actors changed. Many – perhaps most – plays were revised when they were reintroduced after any substantial absence from the repertory, or when they were performed by a company different from the one that originally commissioned the play.

Shakespeare was an exceptional figure in this world because he was not only a shareholder and actor in his company, but also its leading playwright – he was literally his own boss. He had, moreover, little interest in the publication of his plays, and even those that appeared during his lifetime with the authorization of the company show no signs of any editorial concern on the part of the author. Theater was, for Shakespeare, a fluid and supremely responsive medium – the very opposite of the great classic canonical text that has embodied his works since 1623.

The very fluidity of the original texts, however, has meant that Shakespeare has always had to be edited. Here is an example of how problematic the editorial project inevitably is, a passage from the most famous speech in *Romeo and Juliet*, Juliet's balcony soliloquy beginning "O Romeo, Romeo, wherefore art thou Romeo?" Since the eighteenth century, the standard modern text has read,

> What's Montague? It is nor hand, nor foot,
> Nor arm, nor face, nor any other part
> Belonging to a man. O be some other name!
> What's in a name? That which we call a rose
> By any other name would smell as sweet.
>
> (II.2.40–44)

Editors have three early texts of this play to work from, two quarto texts and the folio. Here is how the First Quarto (1597) reads:

> Whats *Mountague?* It is nor hand nor foote,
> Nor arme, nor face, nor any other part.
> Whats in a name? That which we call a Rose,
> By any other name would smell as sweet:

Here is the Second Quarto (1599):

> Whats *Mountague?* it is nor hand nor foote,
> Nor arme nor face, ô be some other name
> Belonging to a man.
> Whats in a name that which we call a rose,
> By any other word would smell as sweete,

And here is the First Folio (1623):

> What's *Mountague?* it is nor hand nor foote,
> Nor arme, nor face, O be some other name
> Belonging to a man.
> What? in a names that which we call a Rose,
> By any other word would smell as sweete,

There is in fact no early text that reads as our modern text does – and this is the most famous speech in the play. Instead, we have three quite different texts, all of which are clearly some version of the same speech, but none of which seems to us a final or satisfactory version. The transcendently beautiful passage in modern editions is an editorial invention: editors have succeeded in conflating and revising the three versions into something we recognize as great poetry. Is this what Shakespeare "really" wrote? Who can say? What we can say is that Shakespeare always had performance, not a book, in mind.

Books About the Shakespeare Texts

The standard study of the printing history of the First Folio is W. W. Greg, *The Shakespeare First Folio* (1955). J. K. Walton, *The Quarto Copy for the First Folio of Shakespeare*

(1971), is a useful survey of the relation of the quartos to the folio. The second edition of Charlton Hinman's *Norton Facsimile* of the First Folio (1996), with a new introduction by Peter Blayney, is indispensable. Stanley Wells, Gary Taylor, John Jowett, and William Montgomery, *William Shakespeare: A Textual Companion,* keyed to the Oxford text, gives a comprehensive survey of the editorial situation for all the plays and poems.

Introduction

PERICLES IS ONE OF SEVEN PLAYS that first appeared in print under Shakespeare's name during his lifetime, but nevertheless were not included in the First Folio – plays that did not, that is, become part of the original Shakespeare canon, despite the fact that they were originally ascribed to Shakespeare. All were included in the second issue of the Third Folio (1664), and continued to be integral to Shakespeare's works until Pope's edition of 1723-25, from which they were banished, though they were subsequently included in Pope's second edition of 1728. The seven plays then definitively disappeared from Shakespeare's works until 1780, when Edmond Malone, the editor who did more to establish our notion of what constitutes Shakespeare than anyone since the editors of the First Folio, added *Pericles,* but not the other six plays, to George Steevens's edition of Shakespeare. The play has since that time retained a firm if anomalous place in the Shakespeare canon, while the other plays from the Third Folio have become the "Shakespeare apocrypha."

The play, then, offers a good index to what, historically, has been seen as authentically Shakespearean. There are undeniably wonderful things in *Pericles,* but excellence has rarely been the crucial test. One of the six plays now considered apocryphal, *The Yorkshire Tragedy,* has long been recognized as a powerful and original Elizabethan drama. To our ears it does not sound much like Shakespeare, but the sound of Shakespeare is not really the test. For example, *King John* and *The Merry Wives of Windsor* do not sound like each other, and neither sounds any more Shakespearean than *The Yorkshire Tragedy;* and *Titus Andronicus* has sounded so little like Shakespeare that many critics

Paul Scofield as Pericles at the Shakespeare Memorial Theatre, Stratford-upon-Avon, 1947, the company's first production of the play since 1900. Directed by Nugent Monck, it omitted the first act and was otherwise cut and rationalized, though Scofield's performance was powerfully effective.

from the eighteenth to the mid-twentieth century declared it spurious. Nevertheless, it remained in the canon, serving for one set of editors as potent evidence that even Shakespeare could write bad plays, and for another that since Shakespeare could not have written so bad a play, the whole notion of the Shakespeare canon was suspect. The first and

second parts of Shakespeare's early history play *Henry VI*
provide a different kind of example: they are clearly collaborations, yet throughout their editorial history they have
remained "Shakespeare." And Shakespeare's final history
play, *Henry VIII*, has for the past hundred years generally
been assumed to be a collaboration with John Fletcher,
though there is no evidence to support this view except the
fact that there are sections of it that do not sound to us like
Shakespeare – or do not sound like what we want Shakespeare to sound like: the sound of Shakespeare has varied
widely from age to age.

Why *Pericles*, then, and not *The Yorkshire Tragedy* (or
The London Prodigal, or *Sir John Oldcastle*, or *Locrine*, or
Thomas Lord Cromwell, or *The Puritan Widow*, the rest of
the apocrypha)? There is no answer to this question outside
the play itself: there is something in it we want to claim for
Shakespeare, something our Shakespeare cannot do without. There were from the beginning, however, problems
about introducing it into the canon. The play was first published in 1609 as a quarto that presents numerous textual
difficulties. The first two acts are stylistically so different
from the rest of the play that they seem to be the work of
someone else; many passages throughout the play are muddled or incoherent, and much that is obviously verse has
been printed as prose. Nevertheless, there is no reason to
believe that this was a "pirated" edition (see Note on the
Text); the King's Men did not subsequently publish a "correct" version of the play, and indeed, at a time when Shakespeare's company was taking systematic legal action to
protect its literary property, it ignored *Pericles*, and the
1609 quarto was reprinted five times before 1635. The
play, both on the stage and in print, was hugely popular –
one of Shakespeare's most popular and widely performed
plays – yet the King's Men never asserted their right to it.
Whether this was because they did not believe it was really
by Shakespeare, or could not provide a satisfactory text for
inclusion in the folio, or (most likely) simply could not

acquire the rights to reprint it, we have no way of knowing; but problematic as the quarto is, it is in fact no more problematic than several other Shakespeare quartos, and differs from them only in that there is no subsequent "good" text for us to compare it with.

The quarto text, then, is the only text. When the editors of the Third Folio included the play in Shakespeare's works in 1664, they had no choice but to reprint the quarto once again. Problematic as it seems to us – and it undeniably presents insurmountable difficulties for a modern editor – in Shakespeare's age it was in most respects a satisfactory text. For example, in 1610 a group of players in Yorkshire were arrested and charged with sedition: they had given performances of *King Lear* and *Pericles,* which the authorities claimed were (or perhaps had had introduced into them) Roman Catholic propaganda – the members of the troupe were Catholic. In their defense the actors replied that their performing texts were the printed quartos of the two plays. Since these had been licensed for publication, they could not be considered seditious. (This was not held to be a sufficient defense – the court took the position that the licensing of plays was a different matter from the licensing of books.) What is significant for our purposes, however, is that these actors found in the First Quarto of *Pericles* a perfectly satisfactory performing script. Much of the difficulty editors have had with *Pericles* has to do with its failure to read like the edited texts of the folio. But its unedited look has much in common with the first quartos of *Hamlet* and *Romeo and Juliet,* and its often baffling textual problems are similar to those of the 1608 First Quarto of *King Lear,* which, for all its confusions, seems to derive from Shakespeare's original draft of the play. I have chosen, therefore, not to emend that archaeology out of it, and have not attempted to turn it into a normative reading text – which would be possible, in any case, only by rewriting it.

The textual confusion does not end with the quarto. There is also a prose version of the story, apparently based on the play. The title page of George Wilkins's *The Painfull Adventures of Pericles Prince of Tyre*, published in 1608, a year before the First Quarto of *Pericles*, declares that it is "the true history of the play of *Pericles*, as it was lately presented by the worthy and ancient poet John Gower." Wilkins's narrative does indeed generally follow the action of the play (though Gower appears nowhere in it after the title page), and gives fuller, or at least rationalized, versions of a number of problematic incidents. However, it also relies heavily on an earlier version of the Pericles story, which had in turn served as a source for the play, Lawrence Twine's translation of a French romance about the life of a hero named Apollonius of Tyre, *The Patterne of Painefull Adventures*, published in 1594. The relation between Wilkins's novel and the play, therefore, is by no means straightforward.* However, similarities in vocabulary and syntax between the play and Wilkins's novel at critical points make it arguable that if the play is a collaboration, Wilkins was Shakespeare's collaborator. Commentators have resisted the suggestion because Wilkins was a writer of little distinction, and they do not like the idea of Shakespeare collaborating with a hack; but the idea is not inconsistent with what we know about the business of theater in Shakespeare's time. The fact that the only Shakespearean collaborator whose name we know is the very distinguished playwright John Fletcher may certainly imply that Shakespeare did not stoop to collaborating with hacks; but it may equally mean only that we do not know much about Shakespeare's collaborators (to say nothing of his feelings about them), since the folio does not acknowledge collaborations. The first two parts of *Henry VI* and *Macbeth* have

---

*The most detailed attempt to reconstruct the putative original play on the basis of Wilkins's novel is by Philip Edwards, in the New Penguin Shakespeare (London, 1976). The argument is most persuasive in the case of I.2, the action of which does seem to have gotten disarranged. See the Note on the Text.

demonstrably non-Shakespearean elements, yet in the folio they are all Shakespeare; whereas the two plays we know he wrote with Fletcher, the superb *Two Noble Kinsmen* and the lost *Cardenio,* were not included in the volume. And of course it is also quite possible that Shakespeare thought better of Wilkins than we do.

It is undeniable that the first two acts of *Pericles* are radically different in style from the rest of the play. Critics who want to insist that the play is all by Shakespeare (as F. D. Hoeniger in the 1963 Arden edition and, though more cautiously, Doreen DelVecchio and Antony Hammond in the New Cambridge edition do) have to assume that the first two acts have suffered egregiously in transmission, even more egregiously than the last three, which also have serious problems. DelVecchio and Hammond conclude by concurring with the Oxford editors that the play is a masterpiece, and therefore the question of who wrote it is "an interesting *but fundamentally irrelevant* aspect of the process of reading and comprehension" (their italics).* I too like the play, but the question of authorship is surely not irrelevant at all, if the whole point is to include the play in a Complete Shakespeare. It is doubtless the case that in its own time the play did enjoy immense popularity because it was a masterpiece – which is to say that, by the standards of the Renaissance stage, it was very good theater. This is not, however, an argument in its favor now; other blockbusters of the Renaissance stage, such as the perennially popular (and anonymous) *Mucedorus,* survive only, barely, in scholarly editions, and there are many very good Renaissance plays – very good even by modern standards – that are rarely read and never performed. The excellence of *Pericles* is not in question, but its excellence is precisely what is fundamentally irrelevant. The play excites

***Pericles,* ed. Doreen DelVecchio and Antony Hammond (Cambridge, England, 1998), p. 15.

whatever interest it enjoys today only because Shakespeare's name is attached to it.

George Wilkins was not a prolific writer; he was by profession an innkeeper, though when his son was born in 1605 he listed himself in the church register as "George Wilkens, Poett" – some doubt has been expressed about whether this can be the same George Wilkins, but we know of no other writer by that name in the period. Wilkins collaborated with William Rowley and John Day in a play called *The Travails of the Three English Brothers* (1607), and in the same year his own play *The Miseries of Inforst Mariage* was performed by the King's Men. The New Cambridge editors find this surprising and declare the play "bad," but surely the King's Men would not have agreed; and in any case, it was sufficiently popular for its published version to go through four editions. To me the play seems interesting and in parts compelling. Wilkins was also an occasional pamphleteer, and appears to have collaborated with Dekker and Heywood, quite respectable writers.

This is a small literary career, but not a contemptible one. I see nothing inconceivable in the idea that Wilkins, having provided the King's Men with a notably successful play, should have tried his hand at another, and produced the first two acts of *Pericles*. It is true that these do not sound much like *The Miseries of Inforst Mariage*, but neither does the rest of *Pericles* sound like *King John;* and in any case, the play in these scenes is trying to sound like Gower. Shakespeare, I suggest, liking the plot and finding Wilkins's first two acts enough to go on with, touched them up and finished the play – I assume that at this point Shakespeare took control. This I propose as my working hypothesis. The textual problems remain, of course, but they are, as I have indicated, very similar to those of the 1608 quarto of *King Lear;* and, as with that text, I see no reason to assume shorthand reporters, auditory errors, or actors with bad memories. Much, if not all, of the difficulty seems to me to reflect the nature of the manuscript copy

the printers had to work with – as with *Lear,* a rough draft
with many revisions, and a handwriting difficult to read.

Let us turn at last to the play. Its principal source is the
story of Apollonius of Tyre in Book 8 of John Gower's
Confessio amantis (The Lover's Confession), a vast collec-
tion of moralized romances written (in English, despite
the title) around 1390. The tale was already ancient and
famous in Gower's time. For Gower it was a moral fable
about the dangers of sinful love and the rewards of virtuous love; but both the tantalizing lasciviousness of Antiochus's incest and the extensive sufferings of Apollonius
far overshadow the ultimate rewards. Shakespeare and his
collaborator preserved a good deal of their original, following and elaborating Gower's plot, and retaining many
of the names, though with the significant exception of
that of the hero. There is no way of knowing why Apollonius became Pericles, but possibly the playwrights wished
to avoid any confusion with Apollonius of Tyana, a mysti-
cal neoplatonic philosopher about whom a large number of miraculous and fantastic tales had developed. To
replace the name Apollonius with that of Pericles, the
Athenian statesman and military hero, was to move the
story, at least by implication, from the world of fantasy
into the world of statecraft and action.*

---

*There are two other significant name changes in the play. Thaise, who is the
daughter in Gower, becomes her mother – Apollonius's wife in Gower is un-
named; the name Marina appears in none of the sources – and Athenagoras
becomes Lysimachus. The latter change, if history is relevant, is not trivial:
Athenagoras was an early Christian philosopher, who wrote a treatise on the
Resurrection, and should therefore be very much in tune with the play. Lysimachus, however, was one of Alexander's generals, who became the ruler of
Macedonia and was notorious for his tyranny and cruelty. Perhaps this is another case in which Pericles fails to see beyond the surface – and perhaps
Jacobean audiences with classical educations did not foresee a happy future
for Marina.

And yet fantasy is an unabashed element of the play, which signals its commitment to the fabulous from the outset by recalling Gower from the grave to narrate it. For Ben Jonson, classicist and rationalist, *Pericles,* far from being a masterpiece, exemplified in its archaism and eclectic extravagance everything that was pernicious about the theater of the age, everything his own drama had undertaken to reform:

> No doubt some moldy tale
> Like *Pericles,* and stale
> As the shrieve's crusts, and nasty as his fish –
>   Scraps out of every dish,
> Thrown forth and raked into the common tub,
>   May keep up the play club.*

Fantasy and eclecticism, however, clearly defined the direction Shakespeare now wanted his drama to take; the play came at the conclusion of the period in which he composed his greatest and most uncompromising tragedies, and almost seems designed as an antidote to them. *Pericles* was apparently written early in 1608,† two or three years after *King Lear,* a year or two after *Macbeth,* within the same year as *Antony and Cleopatra* and *Coriolanus.* If we look ahead, the plays of the following two or three years are *Cymbeline, The Winter's Tale, The Tempest. Pericles,* in its concern with suffering and the extremes of experience, has much in common with *King Lear* – indeed, in one of the most striking moments of the second act, the language suddenly breaks, momentarily, into something that is recognizably the Shakespeare of *King Lear:*

---

*From the *Ode to Himself* on the failure of his play *The New Inn* (1629); the shrieve, or sheriff, was responsible for supplying meals to the poor, out of leftovers "raked into the common tub," which were notoriously unpalatable.

†It was entered in the Stationers' Register on May 20, at which time it was presumably new.

Yet cease your ire, you angry stars of heaven!
Wind, rain, and thunder, remember earthly man
Is but a substance that must yield to you.

(II.1.1-3)

But *Pericles* is unlike *King Lear* in that it is also concerned
with finding a way beyond tragedy, not the least important
element of which is to leave us, dramatically, significantly
uninvolved in Pericles' suffering. *Pericles* might also be seen
as an alternative to that other tragedy of 1608, *Coriolanus,*
a play about a hero as unyieldingly self-sufficient and as-
sured of his own virtue as Pericles is, but in which these
qualities lead only to isolation and destruction. Shakespeare
is markedly kinder to his heroes in the third play of 1608,
Antony and Cleopatra, whose lust and dissipation are allowed to achieve a genuine transcendence through the passion and theatrical genius of Cleopatra, but in which,
nevertheless, death is acknowledged to be real. That is what
is denied in *Pericles,* as it is, though to a lesser extent, in
Cymbeline, The Winter's Tale, and *The Tempest,* which share
with *Pericles* a dramatic reliance on nonrealistic and even
magical modes of action. These plays have, since the late
nineteenth century, been termed "romances," but the cate-
gory really fits only *Pericles,* with its episodic structure and
its hero who defines himself by answering a riddle, and
then travels the world having adventures.

The most striking element in the play dramatically is its
evocation of Gower, not merely to provide a narration but
to insist that its action is the realization of a book. *The Tempest* too keeps its action firmly under the control of a narra-
tor/actor, the magician Prospero, who is its central character,
though the danger that he may lose control of the action is a
real one; but there is no other Shakespeare play that repre-
sents its action as being under the control of an author. It is,
however, to the point that the author is not Shakespeare:
this is, remember, the poet who published his narrative
poems but not his plays, the poet for whom plays were not

books. As for the hero, he moves through the drama as through an allegory, always subordinated to the story's moral. He himself is an excellent literary critic – he solves Antiochus's riddle without difficulty – but all he learns from the experience is the truism that things are not what they seem, that outward beauty is no guarantee of inner worth. This knowledge does not enable him to anticipate the treachery of Dionyza, to whom he entrusts his daughter; it also does not make of him the active and responsible ruler required by Renaissance statecraft. He does not learn and grow; he suffers and mourns, and that is his salvation. The action of the play goes on around him. And in this sense, *Pericles* is not a romance: not a story of the young hero going through the world gaining wisdom and authority through experience and knowledge, but a tale about salvation through submission and abjection, through the patient endurance of suffering – a lesson, in the deepest sense, not for him but for us. This is no doubt what attracted the Roman Catholic actors in Yorkshire to it, as it must have attracted them to *King Lear:* they would have viewed it as a saint's life; and its claims to transcendence are surely also what ultimately earned it its place in the Shakespeare canon.

The opening scene with its incest plot resonates throughout the play. It establishes Pericles' credentials as a hero who solves riddles – the classic model, significantly, is Oedipus – and also explains the necessity for continuous travel. The early tournament scene at Tarsus similarly establishes his credentials as a knight and lover. But subsequently, the play's action is most dramatic in scenes from which the hero is absent, but which nevertheless reflect intensely on him. The resuscitation of Thaisa in Act III obviously owes much to Cordelia's awaking of Lear; it functions here, however, not as a recognition scene, but as an index to the definition of a good ruler. This scene says that political power, if sufficiently informed by virtue and knowledge, approaches ultimate power: it includes even the power over death. Cerimon, natural magician and sage, serves as a moral touchstone in the play; he is the noble and virtuous ruler Pericles might become, but – as far as the action takes us, at least – does not. In Act IV, the plot against Marina, with Dionyza's scheming and Cleon's temporizing, has an intensity that recalls Macbeth and Lady Macbeth before the murder of Duncan. The dramatic development of Marina's defensive eloquence is a masterpiece of economy and wit, as are the extraordinarily vivid and vital brothel scenes; but all these depend precisely on the fact of Pericles' absence. If he abandons his wife and daughter with the best of intentions, he nevertheless abandons them. The final discovery and recognition scenes are unquestionably moving; but they also have a certain predictable, and, in the case of Thaisa, perfunctory, conclusiveness: Pericles' suffering and mourning are over, but also, this is the way the play ends.

All these moments look forward to similar, if more focused and elaborated, elements of the plays of the next three years. Cerimon is the ruler Prospero too should have been but wasn't – the ruler he might eventually become after the end of *The Tempest* and the return to Italy. Marina is the model for *Cymbeline*'s Imogen in a much larger world of rampant sexuality, but also in a much larger world of choice for women. Marina is one of the most forceful and independent women Shakespeare created, but she is simply given by Pericles in marriage to Lysimachus at the play's conclusion. She expresses neither pleasure nor dismay at the match – she does not participate in it at all. Having defined herself and managed her complex life far more impressively than earlier Shakespeare heroines – say, Portia, Rosalind, Helena, Isabella, or Desdemona – she suddenly has no say whatever in her future. Choosing for herself – as her mother, risking her own father's wrath, chose Pericles – is suddenly not an option for this heroine. Indeed, she is given no options at all, not a single line, not a word of rejoicing or even of assent. As for the idea of openly defying her father's will, as Thaisa had been prepared to do (and Desdemona did, and Imogen will do), it has become, at this point in the play, unthinkable. What has happened between Acts I and V? Is the answer perhaps that Shakespeare took over from the author of *The Miseries of Inforst Mariage*? Marina is disposed of just as the articulate, omnicompetent, virtuous, thoroughly admirable, but also manipulative and unmanageable, Paulina is to be at the end of *The Winter's Tale,* married off in silence. It is difficult not to feel that the play, at the end, simply abandons Marina.

Pericles' reunions with his daughter and wife foreshadow Leontes' overwhelming recovery of Perdita and Hermione in the concluding scenes of *The Winter's Tale;* but the women in that play have much more to do: Hermione and the faithful Paulina have been the architects of Leontes' redemption, and Perdita has chosen her own husband, in defiance of both decorum and good sense. Nevertheless, it is a mistake to view *Pericles* merely as a stage in Shakespeare's development. The play has its own artistic integrity, moving with a dramatic rhythm, eloquence, and formal artistry that look neither forward nor back, and are like nothing else in Shakespeare's work.

Pericles was hugely popular in Jacobean times, with Richard Burbage, the leading tragedian of the King's Men, playing Pericles. It was also considered an appropriate entertainment for the court, and was performed at Whitehall Palace in 1619, shortly after Burbage's death, though the king was not present. Its popularity presumably continued throughout the Caroline era, since it was one of the first plays to be revived at the Restoration – or more precisely, on the eve of the Restoration. In the last months of the Commonwealth the actors, who had not legally performed in public for almost two decades, staged productions of *1 Henry IV, Othello, The Merry Wives of Windsor,* and *Pericles;* these were the surefire hits. The new Pericles was Thomas Betterton at the age of twenty-two and at the very beginning of his career; he was soon to become the most famous tragedian of the age, and was especially admired in this role. Two years later, in 1662, Charles II licensed two companies, headed by Sir William Davenant and Thomas Killigrew, to reform and perform the classics of English drama. The major plays were divided between them, and it was Davenant who drew *Pericles*. But despite Betterton's initial success, he does not seem to have performed the role again, and the stage history of the play in the Restoration is a blank. It remained in the repertory of Davenant's company, but no record of performances survives, and that insatiable theatergoer Samuel Pepys, who saw most of what was performed on the London stage in the 1660s, apparently did not see it. It did not suit the taste of the age; more to the point, it could not be reformed so as to do so.

The sole production in the eighteenth century was a version by George Lillo called *Marina,* performed at Covent Garden in 1738. As the title suggests, Marina is now the central character in a much truncated and sentimentalized plot, though the brothel scenes are still present, and not at all sanitized. After a modest success, the production was never revived, and there was then no performance in London for more than a century. But in 1854 the actor-manager Samuel Phelps mounted a very ambitious *Pericles* at Sadler's Wells, a bid to rival the theatrical extravaganzas Charles Kean was producing in this decade at the Princess's Theatre. In Phelps's version, Gower was omitted, and the play became the vehicle for a progression of grand scenic spectacles as the action made its way around the Mediterranean, concluding with a vast moving panorama depicting the view from Pericles' ship as it traveled from Mytilene to Ephesus for the final recognition scene. The production was greatly admired, but Henry Morley remarked, after a detailed and genuinely enthusiastic account of the performance, that it "may be said to succeed only because it is a spectacle."*

Half a century later, in 1900, Frank Benson's company,

Journal of a London Playgoer (London, 1891), p. 84.

then in its twenty-first season at the Shakespeare Memorial
Theatre in Stratford, did a heavily revised *Pericles* directed
by John Coleman; and the play's fortunes with this company (the ancestor of the Royal Shakespeare Company,
which is committed, at least nominally, to doing all of
Shakespeare with some regularity) are a microcosm of its
history. Coleman's success may be gauged by the fact that,
despite a well-received Old Vic production of the complete
text – Gower, brothel scenes, and all – in 1921, the Stratford troupe did not try the play again until 1947, this time
with Paul Scofield in the title role. According to the RSC's
authorized account, "the director, Nugent Monck, cut the
play so that it opened with the shipwreck. His object was to
'get the audience in and out and save on the electricity
bills.'"* Since then the RSC has performed the play five
times. These productions included, in 1958, a (to me in-
comprehensible) Calypso Gower, and in 1969 the actress
Susan Fleetwood – bafflingly – doubling Thaisa and Marina, so that, as one critic observed, the incest that had been
the source of all evil at the play's opening somehow seemed,
at its conclusion, to be the resolution. This was the last time
the RSC tried the play on its main stage.

This is not to say that there have been no successful
modern productions of *Pericles;* but the most compelling
ones in my own experience have been the least ambitious,
ones that did not undertake to transform it but took it on
its own terms, and allowed its formal structure, complex
language, symbolic richness, and romantic archaism to
carry the play. It is a drama that editors and critics have, for
most of the past century, found fascinating, but that the
professional theater for three hundred and fifty years has either ignored or profoundly distrusted.

STEPHEN ORGEL
Stanford University

*Micheline Steinberg, *Flashback: One Hundred Years of Stratford-upon-Avon
and the Royal Shakespeare Company* (RSC Publications, 1985), p. 52.

Note on the Text

THE EARLIEST REFERENCE TO *Pericles* is its entry in the Stationers' Register on May 20, 1608; the wording of the entry implies that the text submitted, by the publisher Edward Blount, was the promptbook. On the same day he also entered *Antony and Cleopatra*. He did not go on subsequently to publish either play. The quarto that appeared in 1609, published by Henry Gosson, does not relate to this entry: Blount did not transfer his rights to Gosson, and there is no separate entry for Gosson's book. This was irregular, but not illegal. Much of what Gosson printed was ephemera, but he was not a piratical printer, and he may simply have been avoiding the registration fee – a fair number of books published in the period have no Stationers' Register entries, and nothing about the quarto suggests that there was anything surreptitious behind it. The failure to register the book would have caused trouble only if Blount had decided to exercise his right. It does mean, however, that the text Gosson published was not the text Blount had entered – that is, that Gosson had some text other than the promptbook. What that text was it is difficult to say. Editors long believed that its confusions and obvious errors indicated a memorial reconstruction of some sort, but more recent editors have felt that similarities with the text of the 1608 quarto of *King Lear* suggest that it derives at least in part from an authorial rough draft. Clearly the printers had great difficulty reading their copy, and from the Second Quarto onward editors have found it necessary to emend merely to make sense of the text. The play appeared in six early quartos: twice in 1609, and in 1611 (Q3), 1619 (Q4), 1630 (Q5), and 1635 (Q6); none of the editions after the first depends on an independent text. The play was not included in the 1623 folio, for reasons that are unclear, but possibly simply because the rights to reprint it could not be negotiated. It was finally included in the second issue of the Third Folio in 1664.

Act I, scene 2 has often been used as a touchstone for the play's textual problems. In the old Pelican edition, James G. McManaway summarized the scene this way:

> Pericles, newly returned from Antioch, enters with his lords, only to dismiss them with his first words. Then he rehearses in soliloquy the danger to himself and his country from Antiochus, who will never rest easy until Pericles be dead. Thought of the situation has plunged him into unaccustomed melancholy. The lords return, wishing him joy and a safe return from his journey, though no such thing has been mentioned. Helicanus interrupts to silence them, rebuke flatterers (though there has been no flattery), speak sharply to Pericles about the duty of kings to heed honest counsel, and ask pardon for his presumption. Again Pericles dismisses the lords, this time with instructions to report on the shipping in harbor. In a brief exchange, he tests Helicanus, then praises him for his candor, and asks his advice. Helicanus tells him to learn to bear with patience his self-imposed griefs. Only then does Pericles disclose that his melancholy is caused by the evil he has discovered in Antioch and the present danger to Tyre and himself. At once Helicanus advises swift flight until death end the peril. Pericles concurs, puts state affairs in order, and starts for Tarsus.

In a classic essay, Philip Edwards, who believed the play's textual problems were attributable to a memorial reconstruction by a reporter with a poor memory who in the case of I.2 had disarranged his notes, suggested a rearrangement of the text somewhat as follows: Pericles enters and is greeted by the lords. Anxious for the safety of Tyre, he sends them to scan the harbor (for ships from Antioch, of course). Then he soliloquizes about the dangers threatening himself and his subjects from Antiochus. Helicanus comes in and chides Pericles for his melancholy, ending with an apology for his plain speech, with the explanation that not frankness but flattery is a crime against a king. Pericles pardons him and explains the reasons for his conduct. The scene ends as in Q, but the lords know nothing about Pericles' intention of going to Tarsus until after his departure.

This is certainly a better scene, and it may well be what the action of the original script looked like. I do not think memorial reconstruction will in fact explain what has happened to the text, but Edwards's essay, "An Approach to the Problem of *Pericles*" (*Shakespeare Survey* 5, 1952), is essential reading for anyone interested in the textual issues. So are the Oxford editors' essay on the play in the Oxford Shakespeare *Textual Companion* (Oxford, 1987) and the textual discussion in the New Cambridge *Pericles*. All of these, needless to say, are in almost total disagreement. Whatever thesis one argues, however, there is clearly no way of turning what survives of *Pericles* into the dramatically normative drama we assume it was originally. And of course it may well be the case that the play was always less normative than we wish it to be.

There follows a list of all substantive departures from Q, with the adopted reading in italics followed by the quarto reading in roman. Unless otherwise indicated, the adopted readings have been suggested by various editors of the play from the eighteenth century to the present. Emendations that merely affect meter, as in the matter of *-ed* endings, are listed only when the quarto text is printed as verse; and there is no attempt to indicate the extensive relineation.

Names of the Actors (adapted from list printed at end of the play in F3)
I.Cho. 39 *a* (F3) of
I.1 18 *rased* racte **23** *the* th' **30** *deathlike* Death like **57** ANTIOCHUS (not in Q) **112** *our* (F3) your **114** *cancel* (F3) counsell **128** *you're* (F3) you **129** *uncomely* untimely
I.2 3 *Be my* By me **20** *honor him* honour **25** *th' ostent* the stint **30** *am once* **41** *blast* sparke **44** *a peace* peace **60** *heaven* (Q2) heaue **70** *Where, as* (Q2) Whereas **78** *seem* seemes **82** *Bethought me* Bethought **83** *fears* (F4) feare **85** *doubt it, as* doo't, as **121** *we'll* will **123** *prince* Prince **s.d.** *Exeunt* Exit
I.3 28 *seas* Sea **30** HELICANUS (Q4) (not in Q)
I.4 13 *[cease not]* (Schanzer) (not in Q) **15** *lungs* toungs **17** *helps* helpers **39** *savors* savers **58** *thou* (Q4) thee **70** *glory's* glories **74** *him's* himnes **78** *On ground's* our grounds **105** *ne'er* neare
II.Cho. 11 *Tarsus* (Q4) Tharstill **12** *spoken* spoken **19** *for* for though **22** *Sends word* Sav'd one **24** *hid intent . . . murder* (Q2) had intent . . . murder (Q corrected) hid in Tent . . . murdred (Q uncorrected) **36** *aught* ought **40** *'longs* long's
II.1 6 *me breath* my breath **12** *What ho, Pilch* What, to pelch **17** *fetch thee* fetch 'th **32** *devours* (F4) devowre **49** *finny* fenny **83** *moreo'er* more; or **91** *your* you **100** *is* (Q2) I **122** *all thy* all **130** *from* Fame **147** *do'ee* do'e (Q corrected) di'e (Q uncorrected) **159** *delightful* delight **166** *equal* a Goale
II.2 4 *daughter* daughter heere **27** *Più . . . fuerza* Pue Per doleera kee per forsa **28** *what's* (Q4) with **30** *pompae* Pompey **53** *furnishèd* furnisht
II.3 3 *To* I **13** *yours* (Q3) your **37** *Yon* You **43** *son's* sonne **50** *poured* (this ed.) stur'd **112** KING (not in Q)
III.Cho. 1 *rouse* (New Cambridge) rout **6** *'fore* from **7** *crickets* Cricket **10** *Where, by* Whereby **13** *eche* each **17** *coigns* Crignes **35** *Yravishèd* Iranyshed **60** *sea-tossed* seas tost
III.1 7 *Thou* then **8** *spit* speat **11** *midwife* my wife **31** *welcomed* welcome **53** *custom* easterne **62** *ore* (this ed.) oare (See OED "ore" 5; the word is not used elsewhere by Shakespeare. Q's "oare," a variant spelling, is usually emended, unnecessarily but possibly correctly, to "ooze," citing as a parallel Alonso's "my son i' th' ooze is bedded," *The Tempest*, III.3.100.) **64** *aye-remaining* ayre remayning
III.2 57 *bitumed* bottomed **94** *warm* warmth
III.3 s.d. *at Tarsus* Atharsus **6** *hurt* hant **28** *unscissored* unsisterd; *hair* heyre (Steevens's emendation for Q's "unsisterd shall this heyre" has been almost universally adopted — Wilkins's prose narrative of the play has Pericles vow "his head should grow unscissored . . . till he had married his daughter" — but if "unsisterd" is correct, then Pericles is saying he will not remarry and provide his heir Marina with a sister. This is far-fetched — concern about a possible brother would make more sense, since Marina would no longer be the heir — but it is not impossible.)
III.4 s.d. *Thaisa* Tharsa **5** *bearing* learning **9** *vestal* (F3) vastall
IV.Cho. 14 *Seeks* Seeke **26** *night bird* night bed **48** *on* one

IV.1 5-6 *or flaming... Enslave* in flaming, thy love bosome, enflame 27 *On... margent* ere the sea marre it 63 *stem* sterne 76 *la* law

IV.2 4 *much* (Q2) much much 72 *pleasure* peasure 100 *i' the* ethe 121 *BAWD* (F3) Mari.

IV.3 1 *are* (Q4) ere 8 *o' th'* ath 11 *'t had* tad 12 *fact* face 15 *nor* not 27 *prime* prince 31 *distain* disdaine 33 *Marina's* (Q2) Marianas

IV.4 8 *i' th'* with 10 *the* (Q2) thy 18 *his* this 29 *puts* put 48 *scene* Steare

IV.5 9 s.d. *Exeunt* Exit

IV.6 s.d. *[Pander, Bawd, and Boult]* Bawdes 3 18 *to-bless* to blesse 34 *dignifies* (Q4) dignities 63 *name't* (F3) name 81 *aloof* aloft 122 *ways* way 124 s.d. *Bawd* Bawdes 129 *She* He 146 *ways* (F3) way 159 *Coistrel* custerell 176 *sew* sow 178 *And I* and 187 *women* (Q3) woman

V. Cho. 8 *twin* Twine 13 *lost* left 20 *fervor* (Q corrected) former (Q uncorrected)

V.1 7 *FIRST SAILOR* 2. Say. 11 *FIRST SAILOR* 1. Say. (Q corrected) Hell. (Q uncorrected) 13 *reverend* reverent 30 *sight. He* sight, hee (Q corrected) sight see (Q uncorrected) 31 *Yet... wish* (Q4) (part of preceding speech in Q) 32 *HELICANUS* (Q4) (this line assigned to Lysimachus in Q) 42 *deafened* defend 45 *with her* her; *is now* now 54 *gods* God 61 *presence* present 65 *I'd* (Q4) I do; *rarely wed* (Q4) rarely to wed 66 *one* on 68 *feat* fate 88 *awkward* augward 97 *You are* your 98 *Here* heare; *shores... shores* shewes... shewes 106 *cased* caste 116 *palace* Pallas 118 *my senses* (Q4) senses 121 *say* stay 126 *thought'st* thoughts 135 *thou them* thou 149 *No motion* Motion 174 *PERICLES* (Q4) Hell. 207 *thou art* (Q4) th'art 219 *doubt* doat 237 *life* like 251 *suit* sleight

V.3 6 *who* (F4) whom 15 *nun* mum 37 *Immortal* (Q4) I, mortall 50 *PERICLES* Hell. 61 *Reverend* Reverent

Epi. 12 *their* (Q4) his; *to th'* the

Pericles
Prince of Tyre

GOWER, *as Chorus*
ANTIOCHUS, *King of Antioch*
PERICLES, *Prince of Tyre*
HELICANUS ⎱ *two lords of Tyre*
ESCANES ⎰
SIMONIDES, *King of Pentapolis*
CLEON, *Governor of Tarsus*
LYSIMACHUS, *Governor of Mytilene*
CERIMON, *a lord of Ephesus*
THALIARD, *a lord of Antioch*
PHILEMON, *servant to Cerimon*
LEONINE, *servant to Dionyza*
MARSHAL
A PANDER
BOULT, *his servant*
FISHERMEN
SAILORS
PIRATES
DAUGHTER OF ANTIOCHUS
DIONYZA, *wife to Cleon*
THAISA, *daughter to Simonides*
MARINA, *daughter to Pericles and Thaisa*
LYCHORIDA, *nurse to Marina*
A BAWD
DIANA
LORDS, LADIES, KNIGHTS, GENTLEMEN,
  MESSENGERS

SCENE: *Coastal lands of the Aegean and
    eastern Mediterranean*]
*

Pericles
Prince of Tyre

I.Cho. *Enter Gower [as Chorus].*

[GOWER]
To sing a song that old was sung,
From ashes ancient Gower is come,
Assuming man's infirmities   3
To glad your ear and please your eyes.
It hath been sung at festivals,
On ember eves and holy days;   6
And lords and ladies in their lives
Have read it for restoratives.   8
The purchase is to make men glorious,   9
Et bonum quo antiquius, eo melius.   10
If you, born in these latter times
When wit's more ripe, accept my rhymes,   12
And that to hear an old man sing
May to your wishes pleasure bring,
I life would wish, and that I might
Waste it for you, like taper light.   16
This Antioch, then: Antiochus the Great

I.Cho. Antioch (the modern Antakya, in Turkey): Antiochus's palace. Impaled heads are displayed on the walls.   **3** *Assuming . . . infirmities* taking on human frailty   **6** *ember eves* the eves before fasting days   **8** *restoratives* tonics, medicine   **9** *purchase* benefit   **10** *Et . . . melius* the older a good thing is, the better it is (proverbial)   **12** *wit's . . . ripe* learning is more sophisticated (than in Gower's time)   **16** *Waste . . . light* consume it for you, like a burning candle

18 Built up this city for his chiefest seat,
    The fairest in all Syria –
20 I tell you what mine authors say.
21 This king unto him took a peer,
    Who died and left a female heir,
23 So buxom, blithe, and full of face
24 As heaven had lent her all his grace;
    With whom the father liking took
    And her to incest did provoke.
    Bad child; worse father – to entice his own
28 To evil should be done by none.
    But custom what they did begin
30 Was with long use accounted no sin.
    The beauty of this sinful dame
32 Made many princes thither frame,
    To seek her as a bedfellow,
    In marriage pleasures, playfellow;
    Which to prevent he made a law –
36 To keep her still, and men in awe –
    That whoso asked her for his wife,
38 His riddle told not, lost his life.
39 So for her many a wight did die,
40 As yon grim looks do testify.
        [Indicating the heads]
    What now ensues, to the judgment of your eye
42 I give my cause, who best can justify.   *Exit.*
                            *

18 *chiefest seat* capital 20 *authors* authorities, sources 21 *peer* mate 23 *buxom* lively; *full . . . face* beautiful 24 *As* as if; *his* its 28 *should* that should 32 *frame* journey 36 *still* always 38 *His . . . not* if he failed to solve Antiochus's riddle 39 *wight* person 40 *yon . . . looks* (on the impaled heads of the unsuccessful suitors; see I.1.35–41) 42 *who . . . justify* you, the spectator, are the best judge of my story

❧ **I.1** *Enter Antiochus, Prince Pericles, and Followers.*

ANTIOCHUS
    Young Prince of Tyre, you have at large received   1
    The danger of the task you undertake.
PERICLES
    I have, Antiochus, and, with a soul
    Emboldened with the glory of her praise,
    Think death no hazard in this enterprise.
ANTIOCHUS
    Music! *[Music plays.]*
    Bring in our daughter, clothèd like a bride
    For embracements even of Jove himself;
    At whose conception, till Lucina reigned,   9
    Nature this dowry gave: to glad her presence,   10
    The senate house of planets all did sit
    To knit in her their best perfections.
       Enter Antiochus' Daughter.
PERICLES
    See where she comes, appareled like the spring,
    Graces her subjects, and her thoughts the king
    Of every virtue gives renown to men.   15
    Her face the book of praises, where is read
    Nothing but curious pleasures, as from thence   17
    Sorrow were ever rased, and testy wrath   18
    Could never be her mild companion.
    You gods that made me man, and sway in love,   20
    That have inflamed desire in my breast
    To taste the fruit of yon celestial tree
    Or die in the adventure, be my helps,

I.1 Antiochus's palace   **1** *at . . . received* fully understood   **9** *Lucina* Roman
goddess of childbirth   **10–12** *Nature . . . perfections* i.e., from her conception to her birth, nature ordained a favorable astrological configuration to
make her perfect and render her presence delightful   **15** *gives* that gives   **17**
curious excellent   **18** *rased* erased

As I am son and servant to your will,
To compass such a boundless happiness.

ANTIOCHUS
Prince Pericles –

PERICLES
That would be son to great Antiochus.

ANTIOCHUS
28   Before thee stands this fair Hesperides,
With golden fruit, but dangerous to be touched;
30   For deathlike dragons here affright thee hard.
Her face, like heaven, enticeth thee to view
32   Her countless glory, which desert must gain;
And which, without desert because thine eye
34   Presumes to reach, all the whole heap must die.
    [Indicating the heads]
Yon sometime famous princes, like thyself,
Drawn by report, adventurous by desire,
Tell thee, with speechless tongues and semblance pale,
38   That, without covering save yon field of stars,
Here they stand martyrs slain in Cupid's wars;
40   And with dead cheeks advise thee to desist
41   For going on death's net, whom none resist.

PERICLES
Antiochus, I thank thee, who hath taught
My frail mortality to know itself,
And by those fearful objects to prepare
This body, like to them, to what I must;
46   For death remembered should be like a mirror,
Who tells us life's but breath, to trust it error.
I'll make my will then, and, as sick men do,

28–30 *Hesperides . . . hard* (the Hesperides, daughters of Hesperus, assisted by a dragon, guarded the golden apples of immortality; to steal the apples was one of the labors of Hercules)   **32** *desert* merit (accented on the second syllable)   **34** *all . . . heap* the entire body   **38** *field . . . stars* (the ceiling of the Globe's stage was painted with stars and the signs of the zodiac, and hence called "the heavens")   **41** *For . . . on* from running into   **46–47** *like . . . breath* (the mirror is held in front of the mouth to detect breathing)

Who know the world, see heaven, but, feeling woe,
Grip not at earthly joys as erst they did,   50
So I bequeath a happy peace to you
And all good men, as every prince should do:
My riches to the earth, from whence they came;
  [To the Princess]
But my unspotted fire of love to you.
Thus ready for the way of life or death,
I wait the sharpest blow, Antiochus.

ANTIOCHUS
Scorning advice, read the conclusion then;   57
Which read and not expounded, 'tis decreed,
As these before thee, thou thyself shalt bleed.

DAUGHTER
Of all 'sayed yet, mayst thou prove prosperous,   60
Of all 'sayed yet, I wish thee happiness.   61

PERICLES
Like a bold champion I assume the lists,   62
Nor ask advice of any other thought
But faithfulness and courage.
  [Reads.]
                    The Riddle.
      "I am no viper, yet I feed
      On mother's flesh which did me breed.
      I sought a husband, in which labor
      I found that kindness in a father.
      He's father, son, and husband mild;   69
      I mother, wife, and yet his child.   70
      How they may be, and yet in two,   71
      As you will live, resolve it you."
  [Aside]
Sharp physic is the last! but, O you powers   73

---

50 *erst* formerly 57 *the conclusion* i.e., the riddle (the end of your speech)
60, 61 *'sayed* assayed, tried 62 *assume . . . lists* enter the field of combat (for
jousting) 69 *son* son-in-law (as his daughter's "husband") 70 *mother* (as
her father's "wife") 71 *How . . . two* how all these may be only two people
73 *Sharp . . . last* the conclusion is strong medicine

74   That gives heaven countless eyes to view men's acts,
        Why cloud they not their sights perpetually
        If this be true which makes me pale to read it?
        Fair glass of light, I loved you, and could still,
        Were not this glorious casket stored with ill.
        But I must tell you, now my thoughts revolt;
80   For he's no man on whom perfections wait
        That, knowing sin within, will touch the gate.
        You are a fair viol, and your sense the strings;
        Who, fingered to make man his lawful music,
        Would draw heaven down, and all the gods, to hearken;
        But being played upon before your time,
        Hell only danceth at so harsh a chime.
        Good sooth, I care not for you.

ANTIOCHUS
        Prince Pericles, touch not, upon thy life,
        For that's an article within our law,
90   As dangerous as the rest. Your time's expired.
        Either expound now, or receive your sentence.

PERICLES
        Great king,
        Few love to hear the sins they love to act.
94   'Twould braid yourself too near for me to tell it.
        Who has a book of all that monarchs do,
        He's more secure to keep it shut than shown;
97   For vice repeated is like the wand'ring wind,
        Blows dust in others' eyes, to spread itself;
        And yet the end of all is bought thus dear,
100   The breath is gone, and the sore eyes see clear
        To stop the air would hurt them. The blind mole casts
102   Copped hills towards heaven, to tell the earth is
            thronged

---

74 *eyes* i.e., stars 94 *braid* upbraid 97–101 *vice ... them* talking about
vice irritates like dust in the eyes, and not only those to whom the vice is reported, but *others* – i.e., the perpetrators; its expensive consequence is that
the vicious see clearly enough to stop the breath of the scandalmongers 102
Copped peaked; *thronged* crushed

By man's oppression, and the poor worm doth die for't. 103
Kings are earth's gods; in vice their law's their will;
And if Jove stray, who dares say Jove doth ill?
It is enough you know; and it is fit,   106
What being more known grows worse, to smother it.
All love the womb that their first being bred.
Then give my tongue like leave to love my head.

ANTIOCHUS *[Aside]*
Heaven, that I had thy head! He has found the mean-   110
  ing.
But I will gloze with him. – Young Prince of Tyre,   111
Though by the tenor of our strict edict,   112
Your exposition misinterpreting,
We might proceed to cancel of your days,   114
Yet hope, succeeding from so fair a tree   115
As your fair self, doth tune us otherwise.
Forty days longer we do respite you;
If by which time our secret be undone,   118
This mercy shows we'll joy in such a son;
And until then your entertain shall be   120
As doth befit our honor and your worth.   121
                          [Exeunt.] Manet Pericles solus.

PERICLES
How courtesy would seem to cover sin,
When what is done is like an hypocrite,
The which is good in nothing but in sight.   124
If it be true that I interpret false,
Then were it certain you were not so bad
As with foul incest to abuse your soul;

---

103 *worm* (any creeping animal, hence an abject creature) 106–7 *fit . . . it*
fitting to smother what grows worse by being widely known 110 *that . . .
head* (1) if only I had your intelligence, (2) if only I could have you beheaded
111 *gloze* be speciously charming 112 *tenor* entire sense 114 *cancel of* the
canceling of 115 *succeeding* proceeding 118 *our . . . undone* i.e., the riddle
be solved 120 *your entertain* our hospitality toward you 121 **s.d.**
Manet . . . solus Pericles remains onstage alone 124 *sight* appearance

128   Where now you're both a father and a son
       By your uncomely claspings with your child
130   (Which pleasures fits a husband, not a father),
       And she an eater of her mother's flesh
       By the defiling of her parents' bed;
       And both like serpents are, who though they feed
       On sweetest flowers, yet they poison breed.
       Antioch, farewell! for wisdom sees, those men
136   Blush not in actions blacker than the night,
137   Will schew no course to keep them from the light.
       One sin, I know, another doth provoke;
       Murder's as near to lust as flame to smoke.
140   Poison and treason are the hands of sin;
141   Ay, and the targets to put off the shame.
       Then, lest my life be cropped to keep you clear,
       By flight I'll shun the danger which I fear.   *Exit.*
       Enter Antiochus.
ANTIOCHUS
       He hath found the meaning,
       For which we mean to have his head. He must
       Not live to trumpet forth my infamy,
       Nor tell the world Antiochus doth sin
       In such a loathèd manner;
       And therefore instantly this prince must die;
150   For by his fall my honor must keep high.
       Who attends us there?
       Enter Thaliard.
THALIARD   Doth your highness call?
ANTIOCHUS
       Thaliard, you are of our chamber, Thaliard,
154   And our mind partakes her private actions
       To your secrecy; and for your faithfulness
       We will advance you, Thaliard.
       Behold, here's poison, and here's gold.

---

128 *son* son-in-law   136 *Blush* who blush   137 *schew* eschew   141 *targets*
shields; *put off* turn aside   154 *partakes* imparts

We hate the prince of Tyre, and thou must kill him.
It fits thee not to ask the reason why.   159
Because we bid it. Say, is it done?   160
THALIARD   My lord, 'tis done.
    Enter a Messenger.
ANTIOCHUS   Enough.
    [To the Messenger]
Let your breath cool yourself, telling your haste.   163
MESSENGER   My lord, Prince Pericles is fled.   *[Exit.]*
ANTIOCHUS   As thou wilt live, fly after; and like an arrow
    shot from a well-experienced archer hits the mark his
    eye doth level at, so thou ne'er return unless thou say
    Prince Pericles is dead.
THALIARD   My lord, if I can get him within my pistol's
    length, I'll make him sure enough. So farewell to your   170
    highness.
ANTIOCHUS
Thaliard, adieu. Till Pericles be dead
My heart can lend no succor to my head.   *[Exeunt.]*
                        ✻

∞ **I.2** *Enter Pericles with his Lords.*

PERICLES
    Let none disturb us.   *[Exeunt Lords.]*   1
                        Why should this change of thoughts,
    The sad companion, dull-eyed melancholy,
    Be my so used a guest as not an hour
    In the day's glorious walk or peaceful night,

---

159 *It . . . not* it is not appropriate for you 163 *Let . . . haste* i.e., as you
pant, tell the reason for your haste
    I.2 Pericles' palace at Tyre (the modern Tyr, in Lebanon) **s.d.** (The en-
trance and immediate dismissal of the lords has been called impossible, but
though there is no parallel for it in Shakespeare, it is a theatrically effective
way of indicating that Pericles has just concluded a public scene and is about
to begin a private one. The scene as a whole, however, may be garbled; see
Note on the Text.) 1 *change of thoughts* i.e., unaccustomed *melancholy*

The tomb where grief should sleep, can breed me
    quiet?
Here pleasures court mine eyes, and mine eyes shun
    them,
And danger, which I feared, is at Antioch,
8   Whose arm seems far too short to hit me here.
Yet neither pleasure's art can joy my spirits,
10 Nor yet the other's distance comfort me.
Then it is thus: the passions of the mind,
12 That have their first conception by misdread,
Have after-nourishment and life by care;
And what was first but fear what might be done,
15 Grows elder now, and cares it be not done.
And so with me. The great Antiochus,
'Gainst whom I am too little to contend,
Since he's so great can make his will his act,
Will think me speaking, though I swear to silence;
20 Nor boots it me to say I honor him
If he suspect I may dishonor him.
And what may make him blush in being known,
He'll stop the course by which it might be known.
With hostile forces he'll o'erspread the land,
25 And with th' ostent of war will look so huge
26 Amazement shall drive courage from the state,
Our men be vanquished ere they do resist,
And subjects punished that ne'er thought offense;
Which care of them, not pity of myself –
30 Who am no more but as the tops of trees,
31 Which fence the roots they grow by and defend them –
Makes both my body pine and soul to languish,
33 And punish that before that he would punish.
    Enter [Helicanus and] all the Lords to Pericles.

---

8 *arm . . . short* (alluding to the proverb "kings have long arms" – cf. "the
long arm of the law")   12 *have . . . misdread* are born of fear   15 *cares* takes
care that   20 *boots it* does it help   25 *ostent* display   26 *Amazement* terror
31 *fence* protect   33 *punish . . . punish* punish in advance him whom Antiochus wishes to punish

FIRST LORD
  Joy and all comfort in your sacred breast!
SECOND LORD
  And keep your mind, till you return to us,
  Peaceful and comfortable.
HELICANUS
  Peace, peace, and give experience tongue.
  They do abuse the king that flatter him.
  For flattery is the bellows blows up sin;   39
  The thing the which is flattered, but a spark   40
  To which that blast gives heat and stronger glowing;
  Whereas reproof, obedient and in order,
  Fits kings as they are men, for they may err.
  When Signor Sooth here does proclaim a peace,   44
  He flatters you, makes war upon your life.
  Prince, pardon me; or strike me, if you please.
  I cannot be much lower than my knees.
    [Kneels.]
PERICLES
  All leave us else; but let your cares o'erlook
  What shipping and what lading's in our haven,   49
  And then return to us. [Exeunt Lords.] Helicanus, thou   50
    hast
  Moved us. What seest thou in our looks?
HELICANUS
  An angry brow, dread lord.
PERICLES
  If there be such a dart in princes' frowns,
  How durst thy tongue move anger to our face?
HELICANUS
  How dares the plants look up to heaven
  From whence they have their nourishment?
PERICLES
  Thou knowest I have power to take thy life from thee.

---

39 *blows* that blows **44** *Signor Sooth* (ironic: "Master Truth") **49** *haven*
harbor

HELICANUS
  I have ground the ax myself. Do but you strike the
  blow.
PERICLES
  Rise, prithee rise, sit down. *[Helicanus rises and sits.]*
  Thou art no flatterer.
60 I thank thee for't; and heaven forbid
61 That kings should let their ears hear their faults hid.
  Fit counselor and servant for a prince,
  Who by thy wisdom makes a prince thy servant,
  What wouldst thou have me do?
HELICANUS   To bear with patience
  Such griefs as you yourself do lay upon yourself.
PERICLES
  Thou speak'st like a physician, Helicanus,
  That ministers a potion unto me
  That thou wouldst tremble to receive thyself.
  Attend me then. I went to Antioch,
70 Where, as thou know'st, against the face of death
71 I sought the purchase of a glorious beauty,
72 From whence an issue I might propagate
73 Are arms to princes and bring joys to subjects.
  Her face was to mine eye beyond all wonder;
  The rest (hark in thine ear) as black as incest;
  Which by my knowledge found, the sinful father
  Seemed not to strike, but smooth. But thou know'st
    this,
  'Tis time to fear when tyrants seem to kiss.
  Which fear so grew in me I hither fled
80 Under the covering of a careful night,
  Who seemed my good protector; and being here,
  Bethought me what was past, what might succeed.
  I knew him tyrannous; and tyrants' fears

---

61 *let . . . hid* i.e., listen to flattery   **71** *purchase* acquisition (not necessarily by buying)   **72** *issue* offspring   **73** *Are arms* which are a source of strength   **80** *careful* (1) watchful, (2) troubled

Decrease not, but grow faster than the years;
And should he doubt it, as no doubt he doth,
That I should open to the listening air   86
How many worthy princes' bloods were shed
To keep his bed of blackness unlaid ope,   88
To lop that doubt, he'll fill this land with arms
And make pretense of wrong that I have done him;   90
When all, for mine, if I may call offense,   91
Must feel war's blow, who spares not innocence;
Which love to all, of which thyself art one,
Who now reproved'st me for't –

HELICANUS   Alas, sir!

PERICLES
Drew sleep out of mine eyes, blood from my cheeks,
Musings into my mind, with thousand doubts
How I might stop this tempest ere it came;
And finding little comfort to relieve them,
I thought it princely charity to grieve for them.

HELICANUS
Well, my lord, since you have given me leave to speak,   100
Freely will I speak. Antiochus you fear,
And justly too I think you fear the tyrant,
Who either by public war or private treason
Will take away your life.
Therefore, my lord, go travel for a while,
Till that his rage and anger be forgot,
Or till the Destinies do cut his thread of life.
Your rule direct to any; if to me,   108
Day serves not light more faithful than I'll be.

PERICLES
I do not doubt thy faith;   110
But should he wrong my liberties in my absence?   111

HELICANUS
We'll mingle our bloods together in the earth,

---

86 *open* reveal 88 *unlaid ope* not revealed 91 *mine* i.e., my offense 108
direct assign 111 *liberties* territorial rights

From whence we had our being and our birth.
PERICLES
    Tyre, I now look from thee then and to Tarsus
    Intend my travel, where I'll hear from thee;
116   And by whose letters I'll dispose myself.
    The care I had and have of subjects' good
    On thee I lay, whose wisdom's strength can bear it.
    I'll take thy word for faith, not ask thine oath.
120   Who shuns not to break one will crack both:
121   But in our orbs we'll live so round and safe
122   That time of both this truth shall ne'er convince,
123   Thou show'dst a subject's shine, I a true prince.
                                        Exeunt.

                    *

∾ **I.3** *Enter Thaliard solus.*

THALIARD   So, this is Tyre, and this the court. Here must
    I kill King Pericles; and if I do it not, I am sure to be
    hanged at home. 'Tis dangerous. Well, I perceive he
    was a wise fellow and had good discretion that, being
    bid to ask what he would of the king, desired he might
    know none of his secrets. Now do I see he had some
    reason for't; for if a king bid a man be a villain, he's
    bound by the indenture of his oath to be one. Husht,
    here comes the lords of Tyre.
        Enter Helicanus, Escanes, with other Lords.
HELICANUS
10   You shall not need, my fellow peers of Tyre,
    Further to question me of your king's departure.
    His sealed commission, left in trust with me,
    Does speak sufficiently he's gone to travel.
THALIARD   *[Aside]* How? the king gone?

---

116 *dispose myself* make my arrangements 121 *orbs* separate worlds 122
of . . . convince shall never deny this truth of us both 123 *shine* radiance
    I.3 Another room in Pericles' palace at Tyre

HELICANUS
    If further yet you will be satisfied
    Why as it were unlicensed of your loves   16
    He would depart, I'll give some light unto you.
    Being at Antioch –
THALIARD   *[Aside]*   What from Antioch?
HELICANUS
    Royal Antiochus, on what cause I know not,
    Took some displeasure at him; at least he judged so;   20
    And doubting lest he had erred or sinned,   21
    To show his sorrow, he'd correct himself;
    So puts himself unto the shipman's toil,
    With whom each minute threatens life or death.
THALIARD   *[Aside]*
    Well, I perceive
    I shall not be hanged now, although I would;   26
    But since he's gone, the king's seas must please: 27
    He scaped the land to perish at the seas.
    I'll present myself. – Peace to the lords of Tyre!
HELICANUS
    Lord Thaliard from Antiochus is welcome.   30
THALIARD
    From him I come
    With message unto princely Pericles;
    But since my landing I have understood
    Your lord has betake himself to unknown travels.   34
    Now message must return from whence it came.
HELICANUS
    We have no reason to desire it,
    Commended to our master, not to us.   37
    Yet, ere you shall depart, this we desire –
    As friends to Antioch, we may feast in Tyre.   *Exeunt.*

---

16 *as . . . loves* without your loving assent   **21** *doubting* fearing   **26** *although . . . would* i.e., even though failing to kill Pericles means a sentence of death   **27** *the . . . please* the seas must do the king's work   **34** *betake himself to* undertaken for himself   **37** *Commended* since it was addressed

*

∾ **I.4** *Enter Cleon, the Governor of Tarsus, with his wife
[Dionyza] and others.*

CLEON
　My Dionyza, shall we rest us here,
　And by relating tales of others' griefs,
　See if 'twill teach us to forget our own?
DIONYZA
　That were to blow at fire in hope to quench it;
5　For who digs hills because they do aspire
　Throws down one mountain to cast up a higher.
　O my distressèd lord, even such our griefs are!
8　Here they are but felt and seen with mischief's eyes,
9　But like to groves, being topped, they higher rise.
CLEON
10　O Dionyza,
　Who wanteth food, and will not say he wants it,
　Or can conceal his hunger till he famish?
13　Our tongues and sorrows [cease not] to sound deep
　Our woes into the air; our eyes to weep
　Till lungs fetch breath that may proclaim them louder;
　That, if heaven slumber while their creatures want,
　They may awake their helps to comfort them.
　I'll then discourse our woes, felt several years,
19　And, wanting breath to speak, help me with tears.
DIONYZA
20　I'll do my best, sir.
CLEON
　This Tarsus, o'er which I have the government,

I.4 The governor's house at Tarsus (in modern Turkey)   **5** *digs* excavates; *aspire* rise too high   **8** *mischief's* misfortune's   **9** *topped* pruned   **13** *[cease not]*
(A plausible emendation proposed by Ernst Schanzer; something is clearly
missing from the passage, which as it stands is nonsense.)   **19** *wanting* when
I lack

A city on whom plenty held full hand,　　　22
For riches strewed herself even in her streets;　　23
Whose towers bore heads so high they kissed the
　clouds,
And strangers ne'er beheld but wondered at;
Whose men and dames so jetted and adorned,　　26
Like one another's glass to trim them by;　　27
Their tables were stored full, to glad the sight,
And not so much to feed on as delight;
All poverty was scorned, and pride so great　　30
The name of help grew odious to repeat.

DIONYZA
O, 'tis too true!

CLEON
But see what heaven can do! By this our change
Those mouths who, but of late, earth, sea, and air
Were all too little to content and please,
Although they gave their creatures in abundance,
As houses are defiled for want of use,
They are now starved for want of exercise.
Those palates who, not yet two savors younger,　　39
Must have inventions to delight the taste,　　40
Would now be glad of bread, and beg for it.
Those mothers who to nuzzle up their babes　　42
Thought nought too curious, are ready now　　43
To eat those little darlings whom they loved.
So sharp are hunger's teeth that man and wife
Draw lots who first shall die to lengthen life.　　46
Here stands a lord, and there a lady weeping;
Here many sink, yet those which see them fall
Have scarce strength left to give them burial.
Is not this true?　　　50

---

22 *held . . . hand* unstintingly poured her gifts　23 *her* the city's　26 *jetted*
strutted　27 *glass . . . them* mirror to dress themselves　39 *savors* mouthfuls
42 *nuzzle up* nurture　43 *curious* exquisite, extravagant　46 *life* i.e., the
other's life

DIONYZA
Our cheeks and hollow eyes do witness it.
CLEON
O, let those cities that of plenty's cup
And her prosperities so largely taste
54   With their superfluous riots hear these tears!
The misery of Tarsus may be theirs.
       Enter a Lord.
LORD
Where's the Lord Governor?
CLEON
Here.
Speak out thy sorrows which thou bring'st in haste,
For comfort is too far for us to expect.
LORD
60   We have descried, upon our neighboring shore,
61   A portly sail of ships make hitherward.
CLEON
I thought as much.
One sorrow never comes but brings an heir
That may succeed as his inheritor;
And so in ours, some neighboring nation,
Taking advantage of our misery,
Hath stuffed the hollow vessels with their power,
To beat us down, the which are down already;
And make a conquest of unhappy me,
70   Whereas no glory's got to overcome.
LORD
That's the least fear; for, by the semblance
72   Of their white flags displayed, they bring us peace
And come to us as favorers, not as foes.

---

54 *superfluous riots* self-indulgent or immoderate revels   **61** *portly sail* stately fleet   **70** *Whereas . . . overcome* where no glory is gained in victory   **72** *white flags* flags of truce

CLEON
   Thou speak'st like him's untutored to repeat: 74
   Who makes the fairest show means most deceit.
   But bring they what they will and what they can,
   What need we leave?   77
   On ground's the lowest, and we are halfway there.   78
   Go tell their general we attend him here,   79
   To know for what he comes, and whence he comes,   80
   And what he craves.

LORD
   I go, my lord.   [Exit.]

CLEON
   Welcome is peace, if he on peace consist;   83
   If wars, we are unable to resist.
        Enter Pericles with Attendants.

PERICLES
   Lord Governor, for so we hear you are,
   Let not our ships and number of our men
   Be like a beacon fired t' amaze your eyes.   87
   We have heard your miseries as far as Tyre,
   And seen the desolation of your streets;
   Nor come we to add sorrow to your tears,   90
   But to relieve them of their heavy load;
   And these our ships you happily may think   92
   Are like the Trojan horse was stuffed within   93
   With bloody veins, expecting overthrow,   94
   Are stored with corn to make your needy bread   95
   And give them life whom hunger starved half dead.

---

74 *him's . . . repeat* one who has never been taught the lesson   77 *What . . .
leave* why do we need to flee   78 *On . . . lowest* i.e., we can't fall lower than
the ground   79 *attend* await   83 *if . . . consist* if peace is his intention   87
amaze alarm (beacon fires were set on coastal hills to signal the approach of
hostile ships)   92 *happily* haply, perhaps   93 *Trojan horse* (The Greek forces
finally ended the siege of Troy by sending, supposedly as a peace offering, a
huge wooden horse to the Trojans. The horse was full of Greek soldiers, who
emerged at night and admitted the invading army.); *was* which was   94
bloody veins i.e., bloodthirsty warriors; *expecting overthrow* awaiting the mo-
ment to overthrow (Troy)   95 *corn* grain

ALL   *[Kneeling]*
    The gods of Greece protect you,
    And we'll pray for you.
PERICLES   Arise, I pray you, rise.
       [They rise.]
    We do not look for reverence, but for love,
    And harborage for ourself, our ships, and men.
100 CLEON
    The which when any shall not gratify,
    Or pay you with unthankfulness in thought –
    Be it our wives, our children, or ourselves –
    The curse of heaven and men succeed their evils!
    Till when – the which, I hope, shall ne'er be seen –
    Your grace is welcome to our town and us.
PERICLES
    Which welcome we'll accept, feast here awhile,
    Until our stars that frown lend us a smile.   *Exeunt.*

               *

  ∾ **II.Cho.** *Enter Gower.*

[GOWER]
    Here have you seen a mighty king
2   His child iwis to incest bring;
    A better prince and benign lord,
4   That will prove awful both in deed and word.
    Be quiet then, as men should be,
6   Till he hath passed necessity.
7   I'll show you those in troubles reign,
    Losing a mite, a mountain gain.
9   The good in conversation,
10 To whom I give my benison,
    Is still at Tarsus, where each man

II.Cho. 2 *iwis* surely **4** *awful* deserving of awe or respect **6** *passed necessity* endured great hardship **7** *those* those who **9** *The good* i.e., Pericles; *conversation* conduct **10** *benison* blessing

Thinks all is writ he speken can;   12
And, to remember what he does,   13
Build his statue to make him glorious.
But tidings to the contrary   15
Are brought your eyes. What need speak I?

Dumb Show.
Enter at one door Pericles, talking with Cleon; all the train
with them. Enter at another door a Gentleman with a letter
to Pericles. Pericles shows the letter to Cleon. Pericles gives the
Messenger a reward and knights him. Exit Pericles at one
door and Cleon at another [with their Attendants].

Good Helicane, that stayed at home,
Not to eat honey like a drone
From others' labors, for he strive   19
To killen bad, keep good alive,   20
And to fulfill his prince' desire,
Sends word of all that haps in Tyre:
How Thaliard came full bent with sin
And hid intent to murder him;
And that in Tarsus was not best
Longer for him to make his rest.
He, doing so, put forth to seas,   27
Where when men been, there's seldom ease;
For now the wind begins to blow;
Thunder above, and deeps below,   30
Makes such unquiet that the ship
Should house him safe is wracked and split,   32
And he, good prince, having all lost,
By waves from coast to coast is tossed.
All perishen of man, of pelf,   35

---

12 *all . . . can* everything he says is holy writ   13 *remember* commemorate
15 *tidings . . . contrary* bad tidings   19 *strive* strives   20 *killen* (Middle English form of "kill" – indicating that Gower is speaking his native language)
27 *doing so* acting accordingly   32 *Should* which should; *wracked* tortured
35 *perishen* (more Middle English); *pelf* goods

36   Ne aught escapend but himself;
        Till fortune, tired with doing bad,
        Threw him ashore, to give him glad.
        And here he comes. What shall be next
40   Pardon old Gower; this 'longs the text.   *[Exit.]*

                              *

∾ **II.1** *Enter Pericles, wet.*

PERICLES
        Yet cease your ire, you angry stars of heaven!
        Wind, rain, and thunder, remember earthly man
        Is but a substance that must yield to you;
        And I, as fits my nature, do obey you.
        Alas, the seas hath cast me on the rocks,
        Washed me from shore to shore, and left me breath
        Nothing to think on but ensuing death.
        Let it suffice the greatness of your powers
        To have bereft a prince of all his fortunes,
10   And having thrown him from your wat'ry grave,
        Here to have death in peace is all he'll crave.
            Enter three Fishermen.
12   FIRST FISHERMAN   What ho, Pilch!
     SECOND FISHERMAN   Ha, come and bring away the nets.
     FIRST FISHERMAN   What, Patchbreech, I say!
     THIRD FISHERMAN   What say you, master?
16   FIRST FISHERMAN   Look how thou stirr'st now! Come
17   away, or I'll fetch thee with a wanion.
     THIRD FISHERMAN   Faith, master, I am thinking of the
        poor men that were cast away before us even now.

------

36 *Ne . . . escapend* and none escaped   40 *'longs . . . text* belongs to the action of the play
    II.1 The shore at Pentapolis (imagined to be in Greece, but in fact the
collective name for the five cities of Cyrenaica on the North African coast, in
modern Libya)   12 *Pilch* (literally, a leather coat; also slang for "theft")   16
Look . . . stirr'st get moving   17 *I'll . . . wanion* I'll beat you with a vengeance

FIRST FISHERMAN   Alas, poor souls, it grieved my heart to   20
hear what pitiful cries they made to us to help them,
when, well-a-day, we could scarce help ourselves.

THIRD FISHERMAN   Nay, master, said not I as much when
I saw the porpoise, how he bounced and tumbled?
They say they're half fish, half flesh. A plague on them,
they ne'er come but I look to be washed. Master, I marvel how the fishes live in the sea.

FIRST FISHERMAN   Why, as men do aland – the great   28
ones eat up the little ones. I can compare our rich mi-
sers to nothing so fitly as to a whale. A plays and tum-   30
bles, driving the poor fry before him, and at last
devours them all at a mouthful. Such whales have I
heard on o' th' land, who never leave gaping till they   33
swallowed the whole parish, church, steeple, bells, and
all.

PERICLES   *[Aside]* A pretty moral.

THIRD FISHERMAN   But, master, if I had been the sexton,
I would have been that day in the belfry.

SECOND FISHERMAN   Why, man?

THIRD FISHERMAN   Because he should have swallowed   40
me too; and when I had been in his belly, I would have
kept such a jangling of the bells that he should never
have left till he cast bells, steeple, church, and parish up
again. But if the good King Simonides were of my
mind –

PERICLES   *[Aside]* Simonides?

THIRD FISHERMAN   We would purge the land of these
drones that rob the bee of her honey.

PERICLES   *[Aside]*
How from the finny subject of the sea   49
These fishers tell the infirmities of men,   50
And from their wat'ry empire recollect   51

---

28 *aland* on land   30 *A* he   33 *heard* . . . *o'* heard of on   40 *Because* i.e., so
that   49 *subject* (1) topic, (2) citizenry   51 *recollect* collect, gather

52 All that may men approve or men detect. –
Peace be at your labor, honest fishermen.
SECOND FISHERMAN   Honest, good fellow? What's that?
55 If it be a day fits you, search out of the calendar, and
nobody look after it.
PERICLES
57 May see the sea hath cast upon your coast –
SECOND FISHERMAN   What a drunken knave was the sea
to cast thee in our way!
PERICLES
60 A man, whom both the waters and the wind
In that vast tennis court have made the ball
For them to play upon, entreats you pity him.
He asks of you that never used to beg.
FIRST FISHERMAN   No, friend? Cannot you beg? Here's
them in our country of Greece gets more with begging
than we can do with working.
SECOND FISHERMAN   Canst thou catch any fishes then?
PERICLES   I never practiced it.
SECOND FISHERMAN   Nay, then thou wilt starve sure; for
70 here's nothing to be got nowadays unless thou canst
fish for't.
PERICLES
What I have been I have forgot to know;
But what I am, want teaches me to think on:
74 A man thronged up with cold; my veins are chill,
And have no more of life than may suffice
To give my tongue that heat to ask your help;
Which if you shall refuse, when I am dead,
78 For that I am a man, pray you see me buried.
79 FIRST FISHERMAN   Die, ke-tha? Now gods forbid't, an I
80 have a gown here; come put it on; keep thee warm.

---

52 *approve* commend; *detect* expose   55–56 *If . . . it* if honesty suits you, don't look for it in the calendar, and nobody else will look for it after you (but the passage is probably corrupt)   57 *May* you may   74 *thronged up* overwhelmed   78 *For that* because   79 *ke-tha* quotha, says he (an otherwise unrecorded dialect form); *an* if

Now, afore me, a handsome fellow. Come, thou shalt   81
go home, and we'll have flesh for all day, fish for fasting   82
days, and moreo'er puddings and flapjacks; and thou   83
shalt be welcome.

PERICLES   I thank you, sir.

SECOND FISHERMAN   Hark you, my friend. You said you
could not beg?

PERICLES   I did but crave.

SECOND FISHERMAN   But crave? Then I'll turn craver   89
too, and so I shall scape whipping.   90

PERICLES   Why, are your beggars whipped then?

SECOND FISHERMAN   O, not all, my friend, not all. For if
all your beggars were whipped, I would wish no better
office than to be beadle. But, master, I'll go draw up the   94
net.   *[Exit with Third Fisherman.]*

PERICLES   *[Aside]*
How well this honest mirth becomes their labor!

FIRST FISHERMAN   Hark you, sir. Do you know where ye
are?

PERICLES   Not well.

FIRST FISHERMAN   Why, I'll tell you. This is called Pen-   *100*
tapolis, and our king the good Simonides.

PERICLES   The good Simonides do you call him?

FIRST FISHERMAN   Ay, sir; and he deserves so to be called
for his peaceable reign and good government.

PERICLES   He is a happy king, since he gains from his
subjects the name of good by his government. How far
is his court distant from this shore?

FIRST FISHERMAN   Marry, sir, half a day's journey. And I'll   108
tell you, he hath a fair daughter, and tomorrow is her

---

81 *afore me* assuredly (a mild oath)   **82** *flesh . . . day* meat for every day   **83**
puddings sausages   **89** *I'll . . . craver* i.e., I'll call myself a craver rather than a
beggar   **90** *scape whipping* (the standard punishment for begging in Jacobean England was a whipping)   **94** *beadle* the church officer who admin-
isters punishments (the point is that he would never lack for work)   **108**
Marry (a mild oath; originally an oath on the name of the Virgin Mary)

110 birthday, and there are princes and knights come from
111 all parts of the world to joust and tourney for her love.

PERICLES   Were my fortunes equal to my desires, I could
113 wish to make one there.

FIRST FISHERMAN   O, sir, things must be as they may;
115 and what a man cannot get, he may lawfully deal for
his wife's soul.

Enter the two [other] Fishermen, drawing up a net.

SECOND FISHERMAN   Help, master, help! Here's a fish
hangs in the net like a poor man's right in the law.
119 'Twill hardly come out. Ha! bots on't! 'tis come at last,
120 and 'tis turned to a rusty armor.

PERICLES
An armor, friends? I pray you let me see it.
Thanks, fortune, yet, that, after all thy crosses,
123 Thou givest me somewhat to repair myself,
And though it was mine own, part of my heritage
Which my dead father did bequeath to me,
With this strict charge, even as he left his life,
"Keep it, my Pericles. It hath been a shield
128 'Twixt me and death," and pointed to this brace,
"For that it saved me, keep it. In like necessity,
130 The which the gods protect thee from, may defend
thee."
131 It kept where I kept, I so dearly loved it;
Till the rough seas, that spares not any man,
Took it in rage; though, calmed, have given't again.
I thank thee for't. My shipwreck now's no ill,
135 Since I have here my father gave in his will.

FIRST FISHERMAN   What mean you, sir?

---

111 *joust and tourney* compete on horseback in a tournament   113 *make one*
be one of the participants   115–16 *deal . . . soul* i.e., get rich by farming his
wife out to other men   119 *bots* a plague (literally, a disease of horses)   123
somewhat to repair something to restore   128 *brace* arm piece   131 *kept*
stayed   135 *my father gave* what my father gave

PERICLES
　To beg of you, kind friends, this coat of worth,　　　　137
　For it was sometime target to a king.　　　　　　　　138
　I know it by this mark. He loved me dearly,
　And for his sake I wish the having of it;　　　　　　　140
　And that you'd guide me to your sovereign's court,
　Where with it I may appear a gentleman;
　And if that ever my low fortune's better,
　I'll pay your bounties; till then rest your debtor.　　　144
FIRST FISHERMAN　Why, wilt thou tourney for the lady?
PERICLES
　I'll show the virtue I have borne in arms.　　　　　　　146
FIRST FISHERMAN　Why, do'ee take it, and the gods give
　thee good on't!
SECOND FISHERMAN　Ay, but hark you, my friend, 'twas
　we that made up this garment through the rough seams　150
　of the waters. There are certain condolements, certain　151
　vails. I hope, sir, if you thrive, you'll remember from　152
　whence you had it.
PERICLES
　Believe't, I will.
　By your furtherance I am clothed in steel;
　And, spite of all the rupture of the sea,　　　　　　　156
　This jewel holds his building on my arm.　　　　　　　157
　Unto thy value I will mount myself　　　　　　　　　158
　Upon a courser whose delightful steps　　　　　　　　159
　Shall make the gazer joy to see him tread.　　　　　　160
　Only, my friend, I yet am unprovided

---

137 *coat of worth* i.e., the armor 138 *target* literally, shield (used metonymically for the whole suit of armor) 144 *pay your bounties* repay your kindness 146 *virtue* strength, courage 150 *made up* put together (the term for tailoring a suit) 151 *condolements* shares due (a malapropism, from "dole") 152 *vails* (1) rewards, tips, (2) tailors' remnants 156 *rupture* violence 157 *jewel* i.e., the armor; *his building* its fixed place 158 *Unto . . . value* i.e., as high as the value of the *jewel* 159 *courser* tournament horse

162   Of a pair of bases.

SECOND FISHERMAN   We'll sure provide. Thou shalt have
my best gown to make thee a pair; and I'll bring thee to
the court myself.

PERICLES

166   Then honor be but equal to my will,
    This day I'll rise, or else add ill to ill.   *[Exeunt.]*

*

∽ **II.2** *Enter [King] Simonides, with Attendants, and
Thaisa.*

KING

    Are the knights ready to begin the triumph?

FIRST LORD

    They are, my liege,

3   And stay your coming to present themselves.

KING

4   Return them, we are ready; and our daughter,
    In honor of whose birth these triumphs are,

6   Sits here like beauty's child, whom nature gat
    For men to see, and seeing wonder at.   *[Exit Lord.]*

THAISA

    It pleaseth you, my royal father, to express
    My commendations great, whose merit's less.

KING

10   It's fit it should be so, for princes are
    A model which heaven makes like to itself.
    As jewels lose their glory if neglected,
    So princes their renowns if not respected.

14   'Tis now your honor, daughter, to entertain

15   The labor of each knight in his device.

---

162 *bases* armed skirts 166 *honor* i.e., the honor I attain
    II.2 Pentapolis: the jousting pavilion at King Simonides' palace 3 *stay*
await 4 *Return* answer 6 *gat* begot 14 *entertain* receive 15 *device* impresa, heraldic shield with its symbol and motto

THAISA
> Which, to preserve mine honor, I'll perform.
> *The First Knight passes by [and his Squire shows his*
> *shield to the Princess].*

KING
> Who is the first that doth prefer himself?   17

THAISA
> A knight of Sparta, my renownèd father;
> And the device he bears upon his shield
> Is a black Ethiop reaching at the sun;   20
> The word, "Lux tua vita mihi."   21

KING
> He loves you well that holds his life of you.
> *The Second Knight.*
> Who is the second that presents himself?

THAISA
> A prince of Macedon, my royal father;
> And the device he bears upon his shield
> Is an armed knight that's conquered by a lady;
> The motto thus in Spanish, "Più por dulzura que por   27
> fuerza."
> *Third Knight.*

KING
> And what's the third?

THAISA   The third of Antioch;
> And his device, a wreath of chivalry;   29
> The word, "Me pompae provexit apex."   30
> *Fourth Knight.*

KING
> What is the fourth?

THAISA
> A burning torch that's turnèd upside down;

---

17 *prefer* present   21 *word* motto; *Lux . . . mihi* your light is life to me   27
Più . . . fuerza more by gentleness than force (a mixture of Italian and Span-
ish)   29 *wreath of chivalry* heraldic chaplet or crown   30 *Me . . . apex* the
triumph's crown has led me on

33   The word, "Qui me alit, me extinguit."
        KING
34   Which shows that beauty hath his power and will,
        Which can as well inflame as it can kill.
            Fifth Knight.
        THAISA
        The fifth, an hand environèd with clouds,
37   Holding out gold that's by the touchstone tried;
38   The motto thus, "Sic spectanda fides."
            Sixth Knight [Pericles].
        KING
        And what's
40   The sixth and last, the which the knight himself
        With such a graceful courtesy delivered?
        THAISA
        He seems to be a stranger; but his present is
        A withered branch that's only green at top;
44   The motto, "In hac spe vivo."
        KING
        A pretty moral.
        From the dejected state wherein he is
        He hopes by you his fortunes yet may flourish.
        FIRST LORD
        He had need mean better than his outward show
49   Can any way speak in his just commend;
50   For by his rusty outside he appears
51   To have practiced more the whipstock than the lance.
        SECOND LORD
        He well may be a stranger, for he comes
53   To an honored triumph strangely furnishèd.

---

33 *Qui . . . extinguit* who feeds me extinguishes me   34 *his* its   37 *by . . .*
tried i.e., tested and proved genuine (the touchstone is a piece of black
quartz; gold rubbed across it leaves a particular kind of streak)   38 *Sic . . .*
fides thus is faithfulness to be tested   40 *the . . . himself* i.e., Pericles is the
only knight who does not have a squire   44 *In . . . vivo* in this hope I live
49 *commend* commendation   51 *practiced . . . whipstock* used a whip (i.e.,
driven a cart)   53 *furnishèd* equipped

THIRD LORD
    And on set purpose let his armor rust
    Until this day, to scour it in the dust.
KING
    Opinion's but a fool, that makes us scan   56
    The outward habit by the inward man.   57
    But stay, the knights are coming. We will withdraw
    Into the gallery.   *[Exeunt.]*   59
        Great shouts [within,] and all cry "The mean knight!"
                              *

∾ **II.3** *Enter the King [Simonides, Thaisa, Marshal,
    Ladies, Lords,] and Knights from tilting.*

KING
    Knights,
    To say you're welcome were superfluous.
    To place upon the volume of your deeds,
    As in a title page, your worth in arms
    Were more than you expect, or more than's fit,
    Since every worth in show commends itself.   6
    Prepare for mirth, for mirth becomes a feast.
    You are princes and my guests.
THAISA
    But you, my knight and guest;
    To whom this wreath of victory I give,   10
    And crown you king of this day's happiness.
        [Places a wreath on Pericles' head.]
PERICLES
    'Tis more by fortune, lady, than my merit.
KING
    Call it by what you will, the day is yours;

---

56 *Opinion* (invariably considered ignorant or prejudiced in Jacobean England); *scan* judge   57 *by* as standing for (literally, near, almost the same as)
59 **s.d.** *mean* humble
    II.3 Simonides' palace   6 *show* performance

And here, I hope, is none that envies it.
In framing an artist, art hath thus decreed,
To make some good, but others to exceed;
17 And you are her labored scholar. Come, queen o' th'
    feast,
For, daughter, so you are; here take your place.
19 Marshal, the rest as they deserve their grace.

KNIGHTS
20 We are honored much by good Simonides.

KING
Your presence glads our days. Honor we love;
For who hates honor hates the gods above.

MARSHAL
Sir, yonder is your place.

PERICLES   Some other is more fit.

FIRST KNIGHT
Contend not, sir; for we are gentlemen
25 Have neither in our hearts nor outward eyes
26 Envies the great nor shall the low despise.

PERICLES
You are right courteous knights.

KING   Sit, sir, sit.
    [Aside]
By Jove, I wonder, that is king of thoughts,
29 These cates resist me, he not thought upon.

THAISA   *[Aside]*
30 By Juno, that is queen of marriage,
31 All viands that I eat do seem unsavory,
Wishing him my meat. — Sure he's a gallant gentleman.

KING *[Aside]*
He's but a country gentleman.
He's done no more than other knights have done;

---

17 *her labored scholar* the pupil who is the product of her labors 19 *the rest*
i.e., seat the other guests 25 *Have* who have 26 *Envies* that which envies
29 *These . . . upon* i.e., I lose my appetite when I don't think about him
(however, perhaps *not* should be "but": his reaction to Pericles would be the
same as Thaisa's in the next speech); *cates* delicacies 31 *unsavory* tasteless

He's broken a staff or so; so let it pass.
THAISA   *[Aside]*
    To me he seems like diamond to glass.
PERICLES   *[Aside]*
    Yon king's to me like to my father's picture,
    Which tells in that glory once he was;   38
    Had princes sit like stars about his throne,
    And he the sun for them to reverence;   40
    None that beheld him but, like lesser lights,
    Did vail their crowns to his supremacy;   42
    Where now his son's like a glowworm in the night,
    The which hath fire in darkness, none in light.
    Whereby I see that Time's the king of men;
    He's both their parent, and he is their grave,
    And gives them what he will, not what they crave.
KING
    What, are you merry, knights?
KNIGHTS
    Who can be other in this royal presence?
KING
    Here, with a cup that's poured unto the brim –   50
    As do you love, fill to your mistress' lips –
    We drink this health to you.
KNIGHTS   We thank your grace.
KING
    Yet pause awhile.
    Yon knight doth sit too melancholy,
    As if the entertainment in our court
    Had not a show might countervail his worth.   56
    Note it not you, Thaisa?
THAISA   What is't to me, my father?
KING
    O, attend, my daughter.
    Princes, in this, should live like gods above,
    Who freely give to every one that come   60

---

38 *tells* shows him   **42** *vail* doff   **56** *might countervail* that could equal

To honor them;
62 And princes not doing so are like to gnats,
Which make a sound, but killed are wondered at.
64 Therefore to make his entrance more sweet,
65 Here, say we drink this standing bowl of wine to him.
THAISA
Alas, my father, it befits not me
Unto a stranger knight to be so bold.
He may my proffer take for an offense,
Since men take women's gifts for impudence.
KING
70 How?
Do as I bid you, or you'll move me else.
THAISA   *[Aside]*
Now, by the gods, he could not please me better.
KING
And furthermore tell him we desire to know of him
Of whence he is, his name and parentage.
THAISA
The king my father, sir, has drunk to you —
PERICLES
I thank him.
THAISA
Wishing it so much blood unto your life.
PERICLES
78 I thank both him and you, and pledge him freely.
THAISA
And further, he desires to know of you
80 Of whence you are, your name and parentage.
PERICLES
A gentleman of Tyre; my name, Pericles;
82 My education been in arts and arms;

62–63 *gnats . . . wondered at* i.e., after the gnats are dead, one wonders that
so small a creature could make so much noise   64 *entrance* reception, entertainment   65 *standing bowl* bowl with a pedestal   78 *pledge him* drink his
health   82 *been* has been

Who, looking for adventures in the world,
Was by the rough seas reft of ships and men
And, after shipwreck, driven upon this shore.

THAISA
He thanks your grace; names himself Pericles,
A gentleman of Tyre,
Who only by misfortune of the seas
Bereft of ships and men, cast on this shore.   89

KING
Now, by the gods, I pity his misfortune   90
And will awake him from his melancholy.
Come, gentlemen, we sit too long on trifles   92
And waste the time which looks for other revels.
Even in your armors, as you are addressed   94
Will well become a soldier's dance.
I will not have excuse with saying this,   96
Loud music is too harsh for ladies' heads,
Since they love men in arms as well as beds.
    They dance.
So, this was well asked, 'twas so well performed.   99
Come, sir, here's a lady that wants breathing too;   100
And I have heard, you knights of Tyre
Are excellent in making ladies trip,   102
And that their measures are as excellent.   103

PERICLES
In those that practice them they are, my lord.

KING
O, that's as much as you would be denied   105
Of your fair courtesy.
    They dance.   Unclasp, unclasp!

---

89 *cast* is cast   **92** *sit . . . trifles* spend too much time on trivial things   **94**
addressed dressed   **96–97** *I . . . heads* I will not accept the excuse that loud
music is too harsh for ladies' ears   **99** *well asked* a good suggestion   **100**
breathing exercise   **102** *trip* (1) dance, (2) misbehave sexually   **103** *measures*
(1) slow dances, (2) rhythmical movements (during sex)   **105–6** *that's . . .
courtesy* i.e., that's as if, out of courteous modesty, you want to be denied a
dance

Thanks, gentlemen, to all; all have done well,
   [To Pericles]
But you the best. – Pages and lights, to conduct
These knights unto their several lodgings. – Yours, sir,
110 We have given order be next our own.

PERICLES
I am at your grace's pleasure.

KING
Princes, it is too late to talk of love;
113 And that's the mark I know you level at.
Therefore each one betake him to his rest;
115 Tomorrow all for speeding do their best.   *[Exeunt.]*
            *

∾ **II.4** *Enter Helicanus and Escanes.*

HELICANUS
No, Escanes; know this of me –
Antiochus from incest lived not free;
3 For which, the most high gods not minding longer
To withhold the vengeance that they had in store,
Due to this heinous capital offense,
Even in the height and pride of all his glory,
When he was seated in a chariot
Of an inestimable value, and his daughter with him,
A fire from heaven came and shriveled up
10 Those bodies, even to loathing; for they so stunk
11 That all those eyes adored them ere their fall
12 Scorn now their hand should give them burial.

ESCANES
'Twas very strange.

HELICANUS   And yet but justice; for though
This king were great, his greatness was no guard

---
113 *mark . . . at* target you aim at   115 *speeding* success
  II.4 Tyre: the governor's house   3 *minding* intending   11 *adored* that
adored   12 *their hand* those whose hands

To bar heaven's shaft, but sin had his reward.   15

ESCANES

'Tis very true.   16

Enter two or three Lords.

FIRST LORD

See, not a man in private conference

Or council has respect with him but he.   18

SECOND LORD

It shall no longer grieve without reproof.   19

THIRD LORD

And cursed be he that will not second it!   20

FIRST LORD

Follow me then. Lord Helicane, a word.

HELICANUS

With me? and welcome. Happy day, my lords.

FIRST LORD

Know that our griefs are risen to the top

And now at length they overflow their banks.

HELICANUS

Your griefs? for what? Wrong not your prince you love.

FIRST LORD

Wrong not yourself then, noble Helicane;

But if the prince do live, let us salute him,

Or know what ground's made happy by his breath.

If in the world he live, we'll seek him out;

If in his grave he rest, we'll find him there   30

And be resolved he lives to govern us,   31

Or, dead, give's cause to mourn his funeral,   32

And leave us to our free election.   33

---

15 *shaft* arrow; *his* its   16 s.d. *two or three Lords* (the vagueness of the stage direction may indicate that the text derives from an authorial manuscript – i.e., from a version of the script before it was put on stage – rather than from a performing copy or promptbook; or it may indicate that the play was performed with a variable number of actors)   18 *he* Escanes   19 *grieve* give offense   31 *be resolved* satisfy ourselves that   32 *give's* give us   33 *election* choice of a successor

SECOND LORD

34   Whose death indeed the strongest in our censure;
And knowing this kingdom is without a head –
Like goodly buildings left without a roof
Soon fall to ruin – your noble self,
That best know how to rule and how to reign,
We thus submit unto, our sovereign.

ALL

40   Live, noble Helicane!

HELICANUS

41   Try honor's cause: forbear your suffrages.
If that you love Prince Pericles, forbear.

43   Take I your wish, I leap into the seas,
Where's hourly trouble for a minute's ease.
A twelvemonth longer let me entreat you

46   To forbear the absence of your king;
If in which time expired he not return,
I shall with agèd patience bear your yoke.
But if I cannot win you to this love,

50   Go search like nobles, like noble subjects,
And in your search spend your adventurous worth;

52   Whom if you find and win unto return,
You shall like diamonds sit about his crown.

FIRST LORD

To wisdom he's a fool that will not yield;
And since Lord Helicane enjoineth us,
We with our travels will endeavor.

HELICANUS

Then you love us, we you, and we'll clasp hands.
When peers thus knit, a kingdom ever stands. *Exeunt.*

                        *

---

34 *Whose . . . censure* his death, indeed, is most likely in our opinion   **41**
Try . . . suffrages follow the path of honor (i.e., remain faithful to Pericles as
rightful ruler): don't give me your votes   **43** *Take . . . . wish* if I accede to
your wishes   **46** *forbear* endure   **52** *Whom . . . return* if you find him and
persuade him to return

II.5 *Enter the King [Simonides], reading of a letter at one door. The Knights meet him.*

FIRST KNIGHT
Good morrow to the good Simonides.

KING
Knights, from my daughter this I let you know,
That for this twelvemonth she'll not undertake
A married life.
Her reason to herself is only known,
Which from her by no means can I get.

SECOND KNIGHT
May we not get access to her, my lord?

KING
Faith, by no means. She hath so strictly
Tied her to her chamber that 'tis impossible.
One twelve moons more she'll wear Diana's livery.   10
This by the eye of Cynthia hath she vowed,   11
And on her virgin honor will not break it.

THIRD KNIGHT
Loath to bid farewell, we take our leaves.
                [Exeunt Knights.]

KING
So they are well dispatched.
Now to my daughter's letter: she tells me here
She'll wed the stranger knight
Or never more to view nor day nor light.   17
'Tis well, mistress, your choice agrees with mine,
I like that well. Nay, how absolute she's in't,
Not minding whether I dislike or no.   20
Well, I do commend her choice and will no longer
Have it be delayed. Soft, here he comes.
I must dissemble it.

II.5 Pentapolis: Simonides' palace   **10** *One . . . livery* i.e., she will remain a virgin twelve months more   **11** *Cynthia* Diana as the moon goddess   **17** *nor day* neither day

Enter Pericles.

PERICLES
All fortune to the good Simonides.

KING
To you as much. Sir, I am beholding to you
For your sweet music this last night.
I do protest my ears were never better fed
With such delightful, pleasing harmony.

PERICLES
It is your grace's pleasure to commend,
30 Not my desert.

KING   Sir, you are music's master.

PERICLES
The worst of all her scholars, my good lord.

KING   Let me ask you one thing: what do you think of
my daughter, sir?

PERICLES   A most virtuous princess.

KING
And she is fair too, is she not?

PERICLES
As a fair day in summer, wondrous fair.

KING
Sir, my daughter thinks very well of you,
Ay, so well that you must be her master,
And she will be your scholar. Therefore look to it.

PERICLES
40 I am unworthy for her schoolmaster.

KING
41 She thinks not so. Peruse this writing else.

PERICLES   *[Aside]*
What's here?
A letter, that she loves the knight of Tyre?
44 'Tis the king's subtlety to have my life. –
O, seek not to entrap me, gracious lord,
A stranger and distressèd gentleman,

---

30 *desert* merit (accented on the second syllable)   41 *else* if you don't believe
me   44 *subtlety* stratagem

That never aimed so high to love your daughter,   47
But bent all offices to honor her.   48
KING
Thou hast bewitched my daughter,
And thou art a villain.   50
PERICLES
By the gods, I have not!
Never did thought of mine levy offense;   52
Nor never did my actions yet commence
A deed might gain her love or your displeasure.   54
KING
Traitor, thou liest!
PERICLES   Traitor?
KING   Ay, traitor.
PERICLES
Even in his throat – unless it be the king –   56
That calls me traitor, I return the lie.
KING   *[Aside]*
Now, by the gods, I do applaud his courage.
PERICLES
My actions are as noble as my thoughts,
That never relished of a base descent.   60
I came unto your court for honor's cause,
And not to be a rebel to her state;   62
And he that otherwise accounts of me,
This sword shall prove he's honor's enemy.
KING
No?
     Enter Thaisa.
Here comes my daughter, she can witness it.
PERICLES
Then, as you are as virtuous as fair,

---

47 *to* as to 48 *bent . . . offices* devoted all my duty 52 *levy* aim at 54
might that might 56–55 *Even . . . lie* i.e., to anyone except the king who
calls me a traitor I reply that he lies in his throat ("to lie in the throat" was
proverbially to tell the worst kind of lie) 60 *relished of* were tainted by 62
her honor's

Resolve your angry father if my tongue
Did e'er solicit, or my hand subscribe
70   To any syllable that made love to you.
THAISA
Why, sir, say if you had, who takes offense
At that would make me glad?
KING
Yea, mistress, are you so peremptory?
(Aside) I am glad on't with all my heart. –
I'll tame you; I'll bring you in subjection!
Will you, not having my consent,
Bestow your love and your affections
Upon a stranger? – *(Aside)* who, for aught I know,
May be, nor can I think the contrary,
80   As great in blood as I myself. –
Therefore hear you, mistress: either frame
Your will to mine; and you, sir, hear you,
Either be ruled by me, or I'll make you –
Man and wife.
Nay, come, your hands and lips must seal it too;
And being joined, I'll thus your hopes destroy,
And for further grief – God give you joy!
What, are you both pleased?
THAISA   Yes, if you love me, sir.
PERICLES
89   Even as my life my blood that fosters it.
KING
90   What, are you both agreed?
BOTH
Yes, if't please your majesty.
KING
It pleaseth me so well that I will see you wed;
And then, with what haste you can, get you to bed.
                                                           Exeunt.

                               *

---

89 *my life* i.e., my life loves; *fosters* nourishes

∾ **III.Cho.** *Enter Gower.*

GOWER
    Now sleep yslackèd hath the rouse;   1
    No din but snores about the house,
    Made louder by the o'erfed breast
    Of this most pompous marriage feast.   4
    The cat, with eyne of burning coal,   5
    Now couches 'fore the mouse's hole;   6
    And crickets sing at the oven's mouth,
    Are the blither for their drouth.   8
    Hymen hath brought the bride to bed,   9
    Where, by the loss of maidenhead,   10
    A babe is molded. Be attent,
    And time that is so briefly spent
    With your fine fancies quaintly eche.   13
    What's dumb in show I'll plain with speech.   14

[Dumb Show.]
Enter Pericles and Simonides at one door, with Attendants; a
Messenger meets them, kneels, and gives Pericles a letter.
Pericles shows it Simonides. The Lords kneel to him. Then
enter Thaisa with child, with Lychorida, a nurse. The King
shows her the letter; she rejoices. She and Pericles take leave
of her father, and [all] depart.

    By many a dern and painful perch   15
    Of Pericles the careful search,
    By the four opposing coigns   17
    Which the world together joins,
    Is made with all due diligence

III.Cho. 1 *yslackèd* slowed, quieted (an archaism); *rouse* drunken revel
4 *pompous* celebratory 5 *eyne* eyes 6 *'fore* before 8 *Are . . . drouth* are
happier because the heat keeps them dry 9 *Hymen* the god of marriage 13
quaintly eche cleverly augment 14 *plain* explain 15 *dern* dreary; *painful
perch* difficult journey (a perch is a measure of land) 17 *opposing coigns* opposite corners

20 That horse and sail and high expense
21 Can stead the quest. At last from Tyre,
22 Fame answering the most strange inquire,
    To th' court of King Simonides
    Are letters brought, the tenor these:
    Antiochus and his daughter dead,
    The men of Tyrus on the head
    Of Helicanus would set on
    The crown of Tyre, but he will none.
29 The mutiny he there hastes t' oppress;
30 Says to 'em, if King Pericles
    Come not home in twice six moons,
32 He, obedient to their dooms,
    Will take the crown. The sum of this,
    Brought hither to Pentapolis,
35 Yravishèd the regions round,
36 And every one with claps gan sound,
    "Our heir apparent is a king!
    Who dreamt, who thought of such a thing?"
    Brief, he must hence depart to Tyre.
40 His queen, with child, makes her desire –
    Which who shall cross? – along to go.
    Omit we all their dole and woe.
    Lychorida her nurse she takes,
    And so to sea. Their vessel shakes
45 On Neptune's billow; half the flood
    Hath their keel cut: but fortune, moved,
47 Varies again; the grizzled north
    Disgorges such a tempest forth
    That, as a duck for life that dives,
50 So up and down the poor ship drives.
51 The lady shrieks, and, well-a-near,

21 *stead* aid 22 *Fame . . . inquire* rumor answering the most distant inquiry
29 *oppress* suppress 32 *dooms* judgment 35 *Yravishèd* enraptured 36 *gan*
sound began to proclaim 45–46 *half . . . cut* i.e., their voyage is half over
47 *grizzled north* gray north wind 51 *well-a-near* alas

Does fall in travail with her fear;   52
And what ensues in this fell storm
Shall for itself itself perform.
I nill relate, action may   55
Conveniently the rest convey,   56
Which might not what by me is told.   57
In your imagination hold
This stage the ship, upon whose deck
The sea-tossed Pericles appears to speak.   *Exit.*   60

                              *

∾ **III.1** *Enter Pericles ashipboard. [Storm.]*

PERICLES
    The god of this great vast, rebuke these surges,   1
    Which wash both heaven and hell; and thou that hast
    Upon the winds command, bind them in brass,
    Having called them from the deep! O, still
    Thy deaf'ning dreadful thunders; gently quench
    Thy nimble sulphurous flashes! – O, how, Lychorida,
    How does my queen? – Thou storm, venomously
    Wilt thou spit all thyself? The seaman's whistle
    Is as a whisper in the ears of death,
    Unheard. – Lychorida! – Lucina, O   10
    Divinest patroness and midwife gentle
    To those that cry by night, convey thy deity
    Aboard our dancing boat; make swift the pangs
    Of my queen's travails!
        Enter Lychorida [with an Infant].
                              Now, Lychorida!
LYCHORIDA
    Here is a thing too young for such a place,

---

52 *travail* childbirth 55 *nill* will not 56 *Conveniently* properly (because it
is appropriate to the stage) 57 *Which . . . told* i.e., what I have related could
not be enacted in a play
    III.1 The deck of Pericles' ship 1 *vast* huge expanse 10 *Lucina* goddess
of childbirth

16   Who, if it had conceit, would die, as I
         Am like to do. Take in your arms this piece
         Of your dead queen.

PERICLES   How? how, Lychorida?

LYCHORIDA
         Patience, good sir; do not assist the storm.

20   Here's all that is left living of your queen,
         A little daughter. For the sake of it,
         Be manly and take comfort.

PERICLES   O you gods!
         Why do you make us love your goodly gifts

24   And snatch them straight away? We here below
         Recall not what we give, and therein may
         Use honor with you.

LYCHORIDA

27   Patience, good sir, even for this charge.

PERICLES
         Now mild may be thy life,
         For a more blusterous birth had never babe;

30   Quiet and gentle thy conditions, for
         Thou art the rudeliest welcomed to this world
         That ever was prince's child. Happy what follows!
         Thou hast as chiding a nativity
         As fire, air, water, earth, and heaven can make,
         To herald thee from the womb.

36   Even at the first thy loss is more than can
37   Thy portage quit with all thou canst find here.
         Now the good gods throw their best eyes upon't.
           Enter two Sailors.

FIRST SAILOR   What courage, sir? God save you.

---

16 *conceit* understanding   24–26 *We . . . you* we do not renege on what we
give to you (our worship, our sacrifices), and thereby deal honorably with
you (as you do not do with us)   27 *for . . . charge* for the sake of this infant
36–37 *Even . . . here* i.e., your loss at the outset is greater than the rest of
your life can compensate   37 *portage* literally, cargo; *quit* requite

PERICLES
　　Courage enough. I do not fear the flaw;　　　　　　40
　　It hath done to me the worst. Yet for the love
　　Of this poor infant, this fresh new seafarer,
　　I would it would be quiet.
FIRST SAILOR　Slack the bolins there! Thou wilt not, wilt　44
　　thou? Blow, and split thyself.
SECOND SAILOR　But sea room, an the brine and cloudy　46
　　billow kiss the moon, I care not.
FIRST SAILOR　Sir, your queen must overboard. The sea
　　works high, the wind is loud, and will not lie till the　49
　　ship be cleared of the dead.　　　　　　　　　　　50
PERICLES　That's your superstition.
FIRST SAILOR　Pardon us, sir. With us at sea it hath been
　　still observed, and we are strong in custom. Therefore　53
　　briefly yield 'er.
PERICLES　As you think meet. Most wretched queen; for
　　she must overboard straight.
LYCHORIDA　Here she lies, sir.　　　　　　　　　　　57
　　　[Reveals the body of Thaisa.]
PERICLES
　　A terrible childbed hast thou had, my dear;
　　No light, no fire. Th' unfriendly elements
　　Forgot thee utterly; nor have I time　　　　　　　60
　　To give thee hallowed to thy grave, but straight
　　Must cast thee, scarcely coffined, in ore;　　　　　62
　　Where, for a monument upon thy bones　　　　　　63

---

40 *flaw* storm (literally, gust of wind)　**44** *bolins* bowlines, the ropes controlling the sails; *Thou . . . not* i.e., be quiet (addressed to the storm)　**46** *But sea
room* so long as we have room to maneuver the ship without running
aground; *an* if　**49** *works high* is very turbulent; *lie* subside　**53** *still* always
57 **s.d.** (Thaisa's body must be produced somehow. The simplest means
would be for Lychorida to draw aside the curtain of the discovery place; a
more awkward and less likely alternative would be for Lychorida to exit and
return with sailors carrying the body.)　**62** *ore* seaweed (see Note on the
Text)　**63** *for* instead of

64   And aye-remaining lamps, the belching whale
        And humming water must o'erwhelm thy corpse,
        Lying with simple shells. O Lychorida,
67   Bid Nestor bring me spices, ink and taper,
        My casket and my jewels; and bid Nicander
69   Bring me the satin coffin. Lay the babe
70   Upon the pillow. Hie thee, whiles I say
71   A priestly farewell to her. Suddenly, woman.
                                   [Exit Lychorida.]

SECOND SAILOR   Sir, we have a chest beneath the hatches,
73   caulked and bitumed ready.
PERICLES
     I thank thee. Mariner, say, what coast is this?
SECOND SAILOR   We are near Tarsus.
PERICLES
     Thither, gentle mariner,
77   Alter thy course for Tyre. When canst thou reach it?
SECOND SAILOR   By break of day, if the wind cease.
PERICLES
     O, make for Tarsus.
80   There will I visit Cleon, for the babe
        Cannot hold out to Tyrus. There I'll leave it
82   At careful nursing. Go thy ways, good mariner;
        I'll bring the body presently.   *Exit [with Sailors].*

                      *

∾ **III.2** *Enter Lord Cerimon, with a Servant [and*
       another in distress].

CERIMON
     Philemon, ho!
     Enter Philemon.

---

64 *aye-remaining lamps* everburning votive lights; *belching* spouting   67
taper candle   69 *satin coffin* coffer lined with satin   71 *Suddenly* immediately   73 *bitumed* made watertight with bitumen   77 *for Tyre* i.e., which is
now toward Tyre   82 *Go thy ways* go on with your work
     III.2 Cerimon's house in Ephesus (on the coast of Ionia, in modern Turkey)

PHILEMON
  Doth my lord call?
CERIMON
  Get fire and meat for these poor men. *[Exit Philemon.]*
  'T 'as been a turbulent and stormy night.
SERVANT
  I have been in many; but such a night as this
  Till now I ne'er endured.
CERIMON
  Your master will be dead ere you return.
  There's nothing can be ministered to nature
  That can recover him. *[To the other man]* Give this to   9
    the pothecary,
  And tell me how it works.   *[Exeunt all but Cerimon.]*   10
    Enter two Gentlemen.
FIRST GENTLEMAN   Good morrow.
SECOND GENTLEMAN   Good morrow to your lordship.
CERIMON   Gentlemen, why do you stir so early?
FIRST GENTLEMAN
  Sir, our lodgings standing bleak upon the sea,   14
  Shook as the earth did quake. The very principals   15
  Did seem to rend, and all to topple.
  Pure surprise and fear made me to quit the house.
SECOND GENTLEMAN
  That is the cause we trouble you so early;
  'Tis not our husbandry.   19
CERIMON   O, you say well.
FIRST GENTLEMAN
  But I much marvel that your lordship,   20
  Having rich tire about you, should at these early hours   21
  Shake off the golden slumber of repose.
  'Tis most strange

---

9 *pothecary* apothecary, druggist   14 *bleak upon* exposed to   15 *as* as if;
principals rafters   19 *husbandry* industriousness   21 *Having . . . you* living
in such luxury (*tire* = attire, and more generally, possessions)

24 Nature should be so conversant with pain,
25 Being thereto not compelled.
CERIMON   I hold it ever
26 Virtue and cunning were endowments greater
Than nobleness and riches. Careless heirs
May the two latter darken and expend;
But immortality attends the former,
30 Making a man a god. 'Tis known, I ever
31 Have studied physic, through which secret art,
By turning o'er authorities, I have,
Together with my practice, made familiar
34 To me and to my aid the blessed infusions
35 That dwells in vegetives, in metals, stones;
And can speak of the disturbances
That nature works, and of her cures; which doth give
    me
A more content in course of true delight
39 Than to be thirsty after tottering honor,
40 Or tie my pleasure up in silken bags,
41 To please the fool and death.
SECOND GENTLEMAN
Your honor has through Ephesus poured forth
Your charity, and hundreds call themselves
44 Your creatures, who by you have been restored;
45 And not your knowledge, your personal pain, but even
46 Your purse, still open, hath built Lord Cerimon
47 Such strong renown as time shall never –
    Enter two or three [Servants] with a chest.
SERVANT   So, lift there.

---

24 *conversant with pain* attentive to trouble   25 *I . . . ever* I have always believed that   26 *cunning* (1) learning, (2) skill   31 *physic* medicine   34 *infusions* liquid extracts   35 *vegetives* plants   39 *thirsty after* eager for   40 *tie . . .
bags* i.e., take my pleasure in acquiring wealth (*pleasure* is usually, pointlessly,
emended to "treasure")   41 *To . . . death* (only fools care about accumulat-
ing wealth, only death ultimately inherits it)   44 *creatures* dependents   45
not not only   46 *still* always   47 (the gentleman is interrupted by the entrance of the servants)

CERIMON   What's that?

SERVANT   Sir, even now did the sea toss up upon our   50
shore this chest. 'Tis of some wreck.

CERIMON   Set't down, let's look upon't.

SECOND GENTLEMAN
'Tis like a coffin, sir.

CERIMON   Whate'er it be,
'Tis wondrous heavy. Wrench it open straight.
If the sea's stomach be o'ercharged with gold,
'Tis a good constraint of fortune it belches upon us.   56

SECOND GENTLEMAN
'Tis so, my lord.

CERIMON   How close 'tis caulked and bitumed.
Did the sea cast it up?

SERVANT
I never saw so huge a billow, sir,
As tossed it upon shore.   60

CERIMON   Wrench it open.
Soft; it smells most sweetly in my sense.

SECOND GENTLEMAN
A delicate odor.

CERIMON
As ever hit my nostril. So, up with it.
O you most potent gods! what's here, a corpse?

SECOND GENTLEMAN
Most strange.

CERIMON
Shrouded in cloth of state, balmed and entreasured   66
With full bags of spices! A passport too!   67
Apollo, perfect me in the characters.   68

---

56 *constraint of fortune* act of will on fortune's part (but *constraint* is probably
incorrect) 66 *cloth of state* here, regal robes (literally, the canopy covering
the royal throne) 67 *passport* then as now, a document providing identifica-
tion and entitling the bearer to safe-conduct through foreign countries 68
Apollo god of medicine and the intellectual arts; *perfect . . . characters* instruct
me in the writing

[Reads.]
          "Here I give to understand,
70   If e'er this coffin drives aland,
          I, King Pericles, have lost
72   This queen, worth all our mundane cost.
          Who finds her, give her burying;
          She was the daughter of a king.
          Besides this treasure for a fee,
          The gods requite his charity."
     If thou livest, Pericles, thou hast a heart
     That ever cracks for woe. This chanced tonight?

SECOND GENTLEMAN
     Most likely, sir.

CERIMON   Nay, certainly tonight,
80   For look how fresh she looks. They were too rough
     That threw her in the sea. Make a fire within.
82   Fetch hither all my boxes in my closet.
                                        [Exit a Servant.]
     Death may usurp on nature many hours,
     And yet the fire of life kindle again
85   The o'erpressed spirits. I heard of an Egyptian
     That had nine hours lain dead,
87   Who was by good appliance recoverèd.
          Enter one with napkins and fire.
88   Well said, well said; the fire and cloths.
89   The rough and woeful music that we have,
90   Cause it to sound, beseech you.
          [Music.]

---

70 *drives aland* is driven to shore 72 *mundane cost* earthly treasure 82
closet private room (the equivalent of "study" or "laboratory") 85 *o'erpressed*
overwhelmed 87 *good appliance* the application of good treatment 88
Well said well done 89 *rough* harsh (in the homeopathic medicine of Renaissance England, diseases were treated by analogy; hence to revive a dying
person with music one provided not lively melodies but deathly ones, to
draw the illness out of the body)

The viol once more. How thou stirr'st, thou block!   91
The music there! I pray you give her air.
Gentlemen, this queen will live;
Nature awakes a warm breath out of her.
She hath not been entranced above five hours.   95
See how she gins to blow into life's flower again.   96
FIRST GENTLEMAN
The heavens through you increase our wonder,
And sets up your fame forever.
CERIMON   She is alive! Behold,
Her eyelids, cases to those heavenly jewels
Which Pericles hath lost, begin to part   100
Their fringes of bright gold. The diamonds
Of a most praisèd water doth appear   102
To make the world twice rich. Live and make us weep
To hear your fate, fair creature, rare as you seem to be.
    She moves.

THAISA
O dear Diana, where am I? Where's my lord?
What world is this?
SECOND GENTLEMAN Is not this strange?
FIRST GENTLEMAN   Most rare.
CERIMON
Hush, my gentle neighbors, lend me your hands.
To the next chamber bear her. Get linen.
Now this matter must be looked to, for her relapse
Is mortal. Come, come, and Aesculapius guide us.   110
                    They carry her away. Exeunt.
                *

---

91 *How . . . block* (always interpreted as Cerimon's indignation at the tardi-
ness of the musician, but it is more likely to be an acknowledgment of the ef-
ficacy of the treatment on the inert but gradually reviving Thaisa)   95
entranced in a trance   96 *gins* begins   102 *water* luster (a technical term for
the fineness of diamonds)   110 *Is mortal* will be fatal; *Aesculapius* the son of
Apollo and patron of medicine

∾ **III.3** *Enter Pericles at Tarsus, with Cleon and
Dionyza [and Lychorida with Marina in her arms].*

PERICLES
    Most honored Cleon, I must needs be gone.
    My twelve months are expired, and Tyrus stands
3   In a litigious peace. You and your lady
    Take from my heart all thankfulness; the gods
5   Make up the rest upon you.
CLEON   Your shakes of fortune,
    Though they hurt you mortally, yet glance
7   Full wonderingly on us.
DIONYZA   O your sweet queen!
    That the strict Fates had pleased you had brought her
        hither
    To have blessed mine eyes with her.
PERICLES
10   We cannot but obey the powers above us.
    Could I rage and roar as doth the sea she lies in,
    Yet the end must be as 'tis. My gentle babe Marina,
    Whom, for she was born at sea, I have named so,
    Here I charge your charity withal, leaving her
    The infant of your care, beseeching you to give her
    Princely training, that she may be mannered as she is
        born.
CLEON
    Fear not, my lord, but think your grace,
18   That fed my country with your corn, for which
    The people's prayers still fall upon you, must in your
        child
20   Be thought on. If neglection should therein make me
        vile,
21   The common body, by you relieved,

III.3 Tarsus **3** *litigious* contentious **5** *shakes* shocks **7** *wonderingly* caus-
ing amazement **18** *corn* grain **20** *neglection* neglect **21** *common body*
populace

Would force me to my duty; but if to that
My nature need a spur, the gods revenge it
Upon me and mine to the end of generation.   24
PERICLES
I believe you. Your honor and your goodness
Teach me to't without your vows. Till she be married,   26
Madam, by bright Diana, whom we honor,
All unscissored shall this hair of mine remain,   28
Though I show will in't. So I take my leave.   29
Good madam, make me blessèd in your care   30
In bringing up my child.
DIONYZA   I have one myself,
Who shall not be more dear to my respect   32
Than yours, my lord.
PERICLES   Madam, my thanks and prayers.
CLEON
We'll bring your grace e'en to the edge o' th' shore,
Then give you up to the masked Neptune and   35
The gentlest winds of heaven.
PERICLES
I will embrace your offer. Come, dearest madam.
O, no tears, Lychorida, no tears,
Look to your little mistress, on whose grace
You may depend hereafter. Come, my lord.   *[Exeunt.]*   40

*

∾ **III.4** *Enter Cerimon and Thaisa.*

CERIMON
Madam, this letter, and some certain jewels,
Lay with you in your coffer; which are   2
At your command. Know you the character?   3

---

24 *the end of generation* my last descendants   26 *to't* to do so   28 *unscissored . . . hair* (see Note on the Text)   29 *show will* appear willful   32 *respect* care   35 *masked Neptune* i.e., Neptune conceals his intentions
     III.4 Ephesus, Cerimon's house   2 *coffer* coffin   3 *character* handwriting

THAISA
    It is my lord's. That I was shipped at sea
5   I well remember, even on my bearing time;
    But whether there delivered, by the holy gods,
    I cannot rightly say. But since King Pericles,
    My wedded lord, I ne'er shall see again,
9   A vestal livery will I take me to,
10 And never more have joy.
        CERIMON
    Madam, if this you purpose as ye speak,
    Diana's temple is not distant far,
13 Where you may abide till your date expire.
    Moreover, if you please, a niece of mine
    Shall there attend you.
        THAISA
    My recompense is thanks, that's all;
    Yet my good will is great, though the gift small.
                                    Exit [with Cerimon].

                        *

∾ **IV.Cho.** *Enter Gower.*

GOWER
    Imagine Pericles arrived at Tyre,
    Welcomed and settled to his own desire.
    His woeful queen we leave at Ephesus,
    Unto Diana there's a votaress.
    Now to Marina bend your mind,
    Whom our fast-growing scene must find
    At Tarsus, and by Cleon trained
8   In music's letters; who hath gained
    Of education all the grace,

---

5 *on my bearing time* at the time when I gave birth   9 *vestal . . . to* I will become a vestal (a priestess devoted to the keeping of the sacred flame of Vesta,
goddess of the hearth)   13 *date* term of life
    IV.Cho.   8 *music's letters* the study of music

Which makes high both the art and place   10
Of general wonder. But, alack,
That monster, envy, oft the wrack   12
Of earnèd praise, Marina's life
Seeks to take off by treason's knife.   14
And in this kind our Cleon hath
One daughter, and a full-grown wench
Even right for marriage sight. This maid   17
Hight Philoten; and it is said   18
For certain in our story, she
Would ever with Marina be.   20
Be't when they weaved the sleded silk   21
With fingers long, small, white as milk;
Or when she would with sharp needle wound
The cambric, which she made more sound   24
By hurting it; or when to th' lute
She sung, and made the night bird mute   26
That still records with moan; or when   27
She would with rich and constant pen
Vail to her mistress Dian still.   29
This Philoten contends in skill   30
With absolute Marina. So   31
The dove of Paphos might with the crow   32
Vie feathers white. Marina gets
All praises, which are paid as debts,
And not as given. This so darks   35
In Philoten all graceful marks
That Cleon's wife, with envy rare,

10–11 *makes . . . wonder* has elevated both the art of music and the general level of wonder **12** *wrack* ruin **14** *treason's* treachery's **17** *right . . . sight* ready to be sought in marriage **18** *Hight* is named **21** *sleded* fine-drawn **24** *cambric* fine linen **26** *night bird* nightingale **27** *still . . . moan* continuously remembers with grief (she recalls the tragedy of her rape and mutilation by her brother-in-law Tereus, and her transformation into a bird; the story is in Ovid, *Metamorphoses,* 6) **29** *Vail* do homage **31** *absolute* impeccable **32** *dove of Paphos* white dove sacred to Venus (Paphos was a city in Cyprus specially favored by her) **35** *darks* darkens

38   A present murderer does prepare
      For good Marina, that her daughter
40   Might stand peerless by this slaughter.
41   The sooner her vile thoughts to stead,
      Lychorida, our nurse, is dead;
      And cursèd Dionyza hath
44   The pregnant instrument of wrath
45   Pressed for this blow. The unborn event
46   I do commend to your content:
47   Only I carried wingèd time
48   Post on the lame feet of my rhyme;
      Which never could I so convey
50   Unless your thoughts went on my way.
      Dionyza does appear,
      With Leonine, a murderer.   *Exit.*

*

❧ **IV.1** *Enter Dionyza with Leonine.*

DIONYZA
    Thy oath remember; thou hast sworn to do't.
    'Tis but a blow, which never shall be known.
3   Thou canst not do a thing in the world so soon
    To yield thee so much profit. Let not conscience,
5   Which is but cold, or flaming love thy bosom
6   Enslave too nicely; nor let pity, which
    Even women have cast off, melt thee, but be
    A soldier to thy purpose.
LEONINE   I will do't.
    But yet she is a goodly creature.

---

38 *present* immediate **41** *stead* assist **44** *pregnant* willing **45** *Pressed* impressed, forced into service **46** *content* pleasure **47–48** *I . . . Post* i.e., my narrative went faster than time **48** *Post* speedily; *lame feet* halting verses

    IV.1 Tarsus, a field **3** *soon* quickly **5** *but cold* i.e., would cool off your ardor **6** *nicely* overscrupulously

DIONYZA
    The fitter then the gods should have her. Here   *10*
    She comes weeping for her only mistress' death.   *11*
    Thou art resolved?

LEONINE
    I am resolved.
      Enter Marina, with a basket of flowers.

MARINA
    No, I will rob Tellus of her weed,   *14*
    To strew thy green with flowers. The yellows, blues, *15*
    The purple violets, and marigolds,
    Shall, as a carpet, hang upon thy grave
    While summer days doth last. Ay me, poor maid,
    Born in a tempest when my mother died,
    This world to me is a lasting storm,   *20*
    Whirring me from my friends.   *21*

DIONYZA
    How now, Marina? Why do you keep alone?   *22*
    How chance my daughter is not with you?   *23*
    Do not consume your blood with sorrowing.
    Have you a nurse of me. Lord, how your favor's   *25*
    Changed with this unprofitable woe.
    Come give me your flowers. On the sea margent   *27*
    Walk with Leonine. The air is quick there,   *28*
    And it pierces and sharpens the stomach.   *29*
    Come, Leonine, take her by the arm, walk with her. *30*

MARINA
    No, I pray you. I'll not bereave you of your servant.

---

11 *only mistress* the one person she cared about, Lychorida 14 *Tellus* the
earth; *weed* garment (of flowers) 15 *thy green* the grass covering the grave
(also, the stage of the Globe and similar theaters was covered with green
rushes during performance) 21 *Whirring* whirling 22 *keep* remain 23
How chance how does it happen 25 *Have . . . me* let me be your *nurse*; *favor*
appearance 27 *sea margent* seashore 28 *quick* fresh 29 *sharpens . . . stomach* increases the appetite

DIONYZA

    Come, come, I love the king your father, and yourself,

33   With more than foreign heart. We every day

    Expect him here. When he shall come and find

35   Our paragon to all reports thus blasted,

    He will repent the breadth of his great voyage;

    Blame both my lord and me, that we have taken

38   No care to your best courses. Go, I pray you.

39   Walk, and be cheerful once again. Reserve

40   That excellent complexion which did steal

    The eyes of young and old. Care not for me;

    I can go home alone.

MARINA   Well, I will go;

    But yet I have no desire to it.

DIONYZA

    Come, come, I know 'tis good for you.

    Walk half an hour, Leonine, at the least.

    Remember what I have said.

LEONINE   I warrant you, madam.

DIONYZA

    I'll leave you, my sweet lady, for a while.

48   Pray walk softly; do not heat your blood.

    What, I must have care of you.

MARINA   My thanks, sweet madam.

                       [Exit Dionyza.]

50   Is this wind westerly that blows?

LEONINE   Southwest.

MARINA

    When I was born the wind was north.

LEONINE   Was't so?

MARINA

    My father, as nurse says, did never fear,

---

33 *With . . . . heart* as if I were a relative   35 *Our . . . reports* what all reports
describe as our ideal   38 *to . . . courses* of what was best for you   39 *Reserve*
preserve   48 *softly* slowly

But cried "Good seamen!" to the sailors, galling   53
His kingly hands haling ropes;   54
And, clasping to the mast, endured a sea
That almost burst the deck.

LEONINE
  When was this?

MARINA
  When I was born.
  Never was waves nor wind more violent;
  And from the ladder tackle washes off   60
  A canvas climber. "Ha!" says one, "wolt out?"   61
  And with a dropping industry they skip   62
  From stem to stern. The boatswain whistles, and
  The master calls and trebles their confusion.

LEONINE
  Come, say your prayers.

MARINA
  What mean you?

LEONINE
  If you require a little space for prayer,
  I grant it. Pray; but be not tedious,
  For the gods are quick of ear, and I am sworn
  To do my work with haste.   70

MARINA   Why will you kill me?

LEONINE
  To satisfy my lady.

MARINA
  Why would she have me killed?
  Now, as I can remember, by my troth,
  I never did her hurt in all my life.
  I never spake bad word nor did ill turn
  To any living creature. Believe me, la,

---

53 *galling* chafing   54 *haling* hauling   60 *ladder tackle* rope ladder in the
rigging   61 *canvas climber* sailor climbing up to the sails; *wolt out* do you
want to get out   62 *dropping* dripping wet

I never killed a mouse, nor hurt a fly.
I trod upon a worm against my will,
But I wept for't. How have I offended
80 Wherein my death might yield her any profit
81 Or my life imply her any danger?
LEONINE
My commission
Is not to reason of the deed, but do't.
MARINA
You will not do't for all the world, I hope.
85 You are well-favored, and your looks foreshow
86 You have a gentle heart. I saw you lately
87 When you caught hurt in parting two that fought.
Good sooth, it showed well in you. Do so now.
Your lady seeks my life; come you between,
90 And save poor me, the weaker.
LEONINE   I am sworn,
And will dispatch.
        Enter Pirates.
FIRST PIRATE   Hold, villain!   *[Leonine runs away.]*
SECOND PIRATE   A prize! a prize!
94 THIRD PIRATE   Half part, mates, half part! Come, let's
95 have her aboard suddenly.
                              Exit [Marina with the Pirates].
        Enter Leonine.
LEONINE
These roguing thieves serve the great pirate Valdes,
And they have seized Marina. Let her go.
There's no hope she will return. I'll swear she's dead
99 And thrown into the sea. But I'll see further.
100 Perhaps they will but please themselves upon her,

---

81 *imply her* implicate her in, cause her   85 *well-favored* good-looking; *fore-show* reveal   86 *gentle* (1) noble, (2) kindly   87 *caught hurt* received a wound   94 *Half part* i.e., divide the spoils   95 *suddenly* instantly   99 *see further* go on watching

Not carry her aboard. If she remain,
Whom they have ravished must by me be slain.   *Exit.*

*

～ **IV.2** *Enter the three Bawds [Pander, Bawd, and
Boult].*

PANDER   Boult!
BOULT   Sir?
PANDER   Search the market narrowly. Mytilene is full of   3
   gallants. We lost too much money this mart by being   4
   too wenchless.
BAWD   We were never so much out of creatures. We have
   but poor three, and they can do no more than they can   7
   do; and they with continual action are even as good as   8
   rotten.
PANDER   Therefore let's have fresh ones, whate'er we pay   10
   for them. If there be not a conscience to be used in   11
   every trade, we shall never prosper.
BAWD   Thou say'st true. 'Tis not our bringing up of poor   13
   bastards, as, I think, I have brought up some eleven –   14
BOULT   Ay, to eleven; and brought them down again.   15
   But shall I search the market?
BAWD   What else, man? The stuff we have, a strong wind
   will blow it to pieces, they are so pitifully sodden.   18

IV.2 Outside a brothel in Mytilene (on the island of Lesbos) **s.d.** *Pander,
Bawd, Boult* (A pander is a male go-between and pimp; a bawd is also a
pimp, generally female, and sometimes a prostitute – the pander and bawd
here are man and wife [see l. 50] and run the brothel; the name of their servant Boult is phallic slang, roughly equivalent to "Shaft" or "Rod": a bolt or
boult is an arrow, a door bolt, or a rolled-up piece of cloth.) **3** *narrowly* care-
fully **4** *gallants* "swingers"; *mart* market time **7** *poor* only **8** *action* sexual
activity **11** *a conscience* ethical behavior **13–14** *'Tis . . . bastards* i.e., rais-
ing bastards isn't enough **14** *as* and **15** *to . . . again* i.e., raised them to the
age of eleven, and then turned them into whores **18** *sodden* literally, boiled,
either in the "stews" (the brothels) or in the sweating tub as a treatment for
venereal disease

19 PANDER   Thou sayest true; there's two unwholesome, o'
20   conscience. The poor Transylvanian is dead that lay
21   with the little baggage.
22 BOULT   Ay, she quickly pooped him; she made him roast
    meat for worms. But I'll go search the market.   *Exit.*
24 PANDER   Three or four thousand chequins were as pretty
    a proportion to live quietly, and so give over.
26 BAWD   Why to give over, I pray you? Is it a shame to get
    when we are old?
28 PANDER   O, our credit comes not in like the commodity,
    nor the commodity wages not with the danger. There-
30   fore, if in our youths we could pick up some pretty
31   estate, 'twere not amiss to keep our door hatched. Be-
    sides, the sore terms we stand upon with the gods will
33   be strong with us for giving o'er.
34 BAWD   Come, other sorts offend as well as we.
    PANDER   As well as we? Ay, and better too. We offend
36   worse. Neither is our profession any trade; it's no call-
    ing. But here comes Boult.
        Enter Boult, with the Pirates and Marina.
    BOULT   Come your ways, my masters; you say she's a vir-
    gin?
40 SAILOR   O, sir, we doubt it not.
41 BOULT   Master, I have gone through for this piece you
42   see. If you like her, so; if not, I have lost my earnest.

19–20 *there's . . . conscience* i.e., two of them *are* diseased, I must admit   **21**
baggage whore   **22** *pooped him* (slang: sexually exhausted him, with the implication that she also infected him with disease–"poop," the rear deck of a
ship, was slang for the anus; it was also used for the vagina, equivalent to the
modern "piece of ass")   **24** *chequins* gold coins (three or four thousand
would have been a fortune)   **24–25** *as pretty . . . over* a nice amount to retire
on, and so give up the trade   **26** *get* earn money   **28–29** *credit . . . danger*
our good name doesn't hold its value as the profit does, and the profit isn't
commensurate with the danger   **31** *hatched* shut (the hatch was a small win-
dow in a door, through which the visitor could be viewed before being admitted)   **33** *strong . . . o'er* a strong argument for us to shut up shop   **34**
sorts kinds of people   **36–37** *Neither . . . calling* our *profession* is neither a le-
gitimate business nor a vocation   **41** *gone through* bargained hard   **42**
earnest down payment

BAWD   Boult, has she any qualities?   43

BOULT   She has a good face, speaks well, and has excellent good clothes. There's no farther necessity of quali-   45
ties can make her be refused.

BAWD   What's her price, Boult?

BOULT   I cannot be bated one doit of a thousand pieces.   48

PANDER   Well, follow me, my masters; you shall have
your money presently. Wife, take her in; instruct her   50
what she has to do, that she may not be raw in her en-   51
tertainment.   *[Exeunt Pander and Pirates.]*

BAWD   Boult, take you the marks of her – the color of
her hair, complexion, height, her age, with warrant   54
of her virginity; and cry, "He that will give most shall
have her first." Such a maidenhead were no cheap
thing, if men were as they have been. Get this done as I
command you.

BOULT   Performance shall follow.   *Exit.*

MARINA
Alack that Leonine was so slack, so slow!   60
He should have struck, not spoke; or that these pirates,
Not enough barbarous, had not o'erboard thrown me
For to seek my mother!

BAWD   Why lament you, pretty one?

MARINA   That I am pretty.

BAWD   Come, the gods have done their part in you.

MARINA   I accuse them not.

BAWD   You are light into my hands, where you are like to   68
live.

MARINA   The more my fault to scape his hands where I   70
was to die.

---

43 *qualities* accomplishments 45–46 *There's . . . refused* there are no other
qualities necessary for lack of which she might be rejected 48 *be . . . doit of*
get the price reduced by a cent less than (a doit was a Dutch coin worth half
a farthing, or an eighth of a penny, hence the smallest possible sum) 50
presently immediately 51–52 *raw . . . entertainment* awkwardly inexperi-
enced in entertaining her clients 54 *warrant* guarantee 68 *are light* have
fallen

BAWD   Ay, and you shall live in pleasure.

MARINA   No.

BAWD   Yes, indeed shall you, and taste gentlemen of all
75   fashions. You shall fare well; you shall have the differ-
76   ence of all complexions. What do you stop your ears?

MARINA   Are you a woman?

78 BAWD   What would you have me be, an I be not a
    woman?

80 MARINA   An honest woman, or not a woman.

81 BAWD   Marry, whip the gosling! I think I shall have
    something to do with you. Come, you're a young fool-
83   ish sapling, and must be bowed as I would have you.

MARINA   The gods defend me!

85 BAWD   If it please the gods to defend you by men, then
86   men must comfort you, men must feed you, men stir
    you up. Boult's returned.

    [Enter Boult.]

88   Now, sir, hast thou cried her through the market?

BOULT   I have cried her almost to the number of her
90   hairs; I have drawn her picture with my voice.

BAWD   And I prithee tell me, how dost thou find the in-
    clination of the people, especially of the younger sort?

BOULT   Faith, they listened to me as they would have
    hearkened to their father's testament. There was a
95   Spaniard's mouth watered, and he went to bed to her
    very description.

BAWD   We shall have him here tomorrow with his best
    ruff on.

BOULT   Tonight, tonight! But, mistress, do you know the
100   French knight that cowers i' the hams?

75–76 *the difference ... complexions* men of every variety 76 *What* why
78 *an* if 80 *honest* chaste 81 *whip ... gosling* i.e., don't be so clueless
(*whip* is a mild expletive, like "drat"); *gosling* young goose (connotes total in-
experience) 81–82 *have ... do* have trouble 83 *bowed* bent 85 *by men*
by providing you with men 86–87 *stir you up* stimulate you 88 *cried her*
advertised her 95 *to her* upon her 100 *cowers ... hams* walks unsteadily;
hams upper legs

BAWD Who, Monsieur Verolles? 101

BOULT Ay, he. He offered to cut a caper at the proclama- 102
tion; but he made a groan at it, and swore he would see
her tomorrow.

BAWD Well, well; as for him, he brought his disease
hither: here he does but repair it. I know he will come 106
in our shadow, to scatter his crowns in the sun. 107

BOULT Well, if we had of every nation a traveler, we
should lodge them with this sign. 109

BAWD *[To Marina]* Pray you come hither awhile. You 110
have fortunes coming upon you. Mark me: you must
seem to do that fearfully which you commit willingly,
despise profit where you have most gain. To weep that
you live as ye do makes pity in your lovers. Seldom but 114
that pity begets you a good opinion, and that opinion a
mere profit. 116

MARINA I understand you not.

BOULT O, take her home, mistress, take her home. 118
These blushes of hers must be quenched with some
present practice. 120

BAWD Thou sayest true, i' faith; so they must; for your 121
bride goes to that with shame which is her way to go
with warrant.

BOULT Faith, some do, and some do not. But, mistress,
if I have bargained for the joint – 125

BAWD Thou mayst cut a morsel off the spit?

BOULT I may so.

---

101 *Verolles* (the name derives from French *vérole*, the pox, syphilis) **102**
offered attempted; *cut a caper* leap up and click his heels (a dance step) **106**
repair renew **107** *crowns . . . sun* ("crowns of the sun" were French gold
coins, but the sun here is Marina; also, a "French crown" was the baldness
symptomatic of syphilis) **109** *this sign* Marina's image **114** *Seldom but*
most of the time **116** *mere* positive **118** *take . . . home* (1) take her inside,
(2) clue her in **120** *present* immediate **121–23** *your . . . warrant* i.e., even
a bride is bashful about doing what she is entitled to do **125** *joint* piece of
meat

BAWD   Who should deny it? Come, young one, I like the
manner of your garments well.

130 BOULT   Ay, by my faith, they shall not be changed yet.

BAWD   *[Tipping him]* Boult, spend thou that in the town.
132   Report what a sojourner we have; you'll lose nothing by
133   custom. When nature framed this piece, she meant
thee a good turn. Therefore say what a paragon she is,
and thou hast the harvest out of thine own report.

136 BOULT   I warrant you, mistress, thunder shall not so
awake the beds of eels as my giving out her beauty stirs
up the lewdly inclined. I'll bring home some tonight.

[Exit.]

BAWD   Come your ways, follow me.

MARINA
140   If fires be hot, knives sharp, or waters deep,
141   Untied I still my virgin knot will keep.
Diana aid my purpose!

BAWD   What have we to do with Diana? Pray you, will
you go with us?   *Exeunt.*

*

∾ IV.3 *Enter Cleon and Dionyza.*

DIONYZA
Why are you foolish? Can it be undone?

CLEON
O Dionyza, such a piece of slaughter
The sun and moon ne'er looked upon.

132–33 *you'll . . . custom* i.e., you'll get your share of the profits ("the custom" is what customers bring)   133 *piece* masterpiece (punning on the sexual sense)   136–37 *thunder . . . eels* (eels were said to be roused out of the
mud by thunder)   141 *Untied . . . knot* I will preserve my chastity (but "untied" should be "tied": to untie the virgin knot was to take the woman's virginity, as Prospero warns Ferdinand not to "break" Miranda's "virgin knot"
[*Tempest*, IV.1.15] – "untried" would make sense; but if the confusion is
Shakespeare's, such confusion is too revealing, in a play so invested in sexuality, to emend away)
IV.3 Tarsus: Cleon's house

DIONYZA
  I think you'll turn a child again.
CLEON
  Were I chief lord of all this spacious world,
  I'd give it to undo the deed. O lady,   6
  Much less in blood than virtue, yet a princess
  To equal any single crown o' th' earth
  I' th' justice of compare! O villain Leonine!   9
  Whom thou hast poisoned too.   10
  If thou hadst drunk to him, 't had been a kindness   11
  Becoming well thy fact. What canst thou say   12
  When noble Pericles shall demand his child?
DIONYZA
  That she is dead. Nurses are not the Fates,
  To foster it, nor ever to preserve.   15
  She died at night; I'll say so. Who can cross it?
  Unless you play the impious innocent   17
  And for an honest attribute cry out   18
  She died by foul play.
CLEON   O, go to! Well, well,
  Of all the faults beneath the heavens, the gods   20
  Do like this worst.   21
DIONYZA   Be one of those that thinks
  The petty wrens of Tarsus will fly hence
  And open this to Pericles. I do shame
  To think of what a noble strain you are,
  And of how coward a spirit.
CLEON   To such proceeding
  Whoever but his approbation added,   26

---

6 *O lady* (generally emended to "A lady," but it is an apostrophe to Marina,
like "O villain Leonine" in l. 9)   9 *I' th'* . . . *compare* in a fair comparison
11 *drunk to him* toasted him (by drinking the poison first)   12 *fact* crime
15 *it* i.e., life   17 *play* . . . *innocent* impiously play the innocent (by betray-
ing Dionyza)   18 *for* . . . *attribute* to gain a reputation for honesty   21–23
Be . . . *Pericles* i.e., imagine that, as in folktales, the birds will reveal the murder   26–27 *Whoever* . . . *consent* i.e., whoever merely approved the deed
after the fact, even though not consenting to it from the outset

27   Though not his prime consent, he did not flow
28   From honorable courses.
DIONYZA   Be it so, then.
    Yet none does know but you how she came dead,
30   Nor none can know, Leonine being gone.
31   She did distain my child and stood between
    Her and her fortunes. None would look on her,
    But cast their gazes on Marina's face,
34   Whilst ours was blurted at, and held a mawkin,
35   Not worth the time of day. It pierced me through;
    And though you call my course unnatural,
    You not your child well loving, yet I find
38   It greets me as an enterprise of kindness
39   Performed to your sole daughter.
CLEON   Heavens forgive it!
DIONYZA
40   And as for Pericles,
    What should he say? We wept after her hearse,
42   And yet we mourn. Her monument
    Is almost finished, and her epitaphs
    In glittering golden characters express
    A general praise to her, and care in us
46   At whose expense 'tis done.
CLEON   Thou art like the harpy,
    Which, to betray, dost, with thine angel's face,
    Seize with thine eagle's talons.
DIONYZA
49   Ye're like one that superstitiously

27–28 *flow . . . courses* descend from honorable origins   **28** *courses* the flow of a river   **31** *distain* overshadow, outshine   **34** *blurted at* scorned; *mawkin* slattern   **35** *the . . . day* i.e., saying "good day" to   **38** *greets me* appears to me   **39** *sole* only   **42** *yet* still   **46** *the harpy* a voracious monster with the face of a woman and the wings and talons of an eagle   **49–50** *Ye're . . . flies* i.e., you are so superstitiously fearful that when winter kills flies, you protest your innocence

Doth swear to th' gods that winter kills the flies;   50
But yet I know you'll do as I advise.   *[Exeunt.]*

*

∞ **IV.4** *Enter Gower.*

GOWER
Thus time we waste and long leagues make short;   1
Sail seas in cockles, have and wish but for't;   2
Making, to take our imagination,   3
From bourn to bourn, region to region.   4
By you being pardoned, we commit no crime
To use one language in each several clime
Where our scenes seems to live. I do beseech you
To learn of me, who stand i' th' gaps to teach you,   8
The stages of our story. Pericles
Is now again thwarting the wayward seas,   10
Attended on by many a lord and knight,
To see his daughter, all his life's delight.
Old Helicanus goes along. Behind
Is left to govern it, you bear in mind,
Old Escanes, whom Helicanus late
Advanced in time to great and high estate.
Well-sailing ships and bounteous winds have brought
This king to Tarsus – think his pilot thought;   18
So with his steerage shall your thoughts groan   19
To fetch his daughter home, who first is gone.   20
Like motes and shadows see them move awhile.

IV.4   1 *waste* annihilate; *leagues* (a league was about three miles; as a unit of measurement it was never in use in England, and was exclusively literary) **2** *cockles* cockleshells;   *and . . . for't* merely by wishing   **3** *Making* traveling   **4** *bourn* frontier   **8** *stand . . . gaps* fill up the gaps in the action   **10** *thwarting* crossing; *wayward* contrary, hostile   **18** *think . . . thought* (the thought guiding the ship is both Gower's and the audience's)   **19** *with . . . steerage* as he steers; *groan* labor   **20** *first . . . gone* has already left

Your ears unto your eyes I'll reconcile.

[Dumb Show.]
Enter Pericles at one door, with all his train; Cleon and
Dionyza at the other. Cleon shows Pericles the tomb [of
Marina], whereat Pericles makes lamentation, puts on
sackcloth, and in a mighty passion departs. [Then exeunt
Cleon, Dionyza, and the rest.]

    See how belief may suffer by foul show:
24 This borrowed passion stands for true old woe;
    And Pericles, in sorrow all devoured,
    With sighs shot through and biggest tears o'ershow-
      ered,
    Leaves Tarsus and again embarks. He swears
    Never to wash his face nor cut his hairs.
    He puts on sackcloth, and to sea. He bears
30 A tempest which his mortal vessel tears,
31 And yet he rides it out. Now please you wit
    The epitaph is for Marina writ
    By wicked Dionyza.
      [Reads the inscription on Marina's monument.]
    "The fairest, sweetest, and best lies here,
    Who withered in her spring of year.
    She was of Tyrus the king's daughter,
    On whom foul death hath made this slaughter;
    Marina was she called, and at her birth,
39 Thetis, being proud, swallowed some part o' th' earth.
40 Therefore the earth, fearing to be o'erflowed,
41 Hath Thetis' birth-child on the heavens bestowed;
42 Wherefore she does, and swears she'll never stint,

---

24 *borrowed* simulated (by Dionyza and Cleon); *old* long-standing   31 *wit*
know   39 *Thetis* (Thetis was a sea nymph, the mother of Achilles, often
confused, as here, with Tethys, the wife of Oceanus, god of the ocean)   41
Thetis' birth-child (because Marina was born at sea)   42 *she* Thetis/Tethys

Make raging battery upon shores of flint."
No visor does become black villainy   44
So well as soft and tender flattery.
Let Pericles believe his daughter's dead
And bear his courses to be orderèd   47
By Lady Fortune, while our scene must play
His daughter's woe and heavy well-a-day   49
In her unholy service. Patience then,   50
And think you now are all in Mytilene.   *Exit.*

                         ✻

∾ **IV.5** *Enter two Gentlemen.*

FIRST GENTLEMAN   Did you ever hear the like?
SECOND GENTLEMAN   No, nor never shall do in such a
  place as this, she being once gone.
FIRST GENTLEMAN   But to have divinity preached there.
  Did you ever dream of such a thing?
SECOND GENTLEMAN   No, no. Come, I am for no more
  bawdy houses. Shall's go hear the vestals sing?
FIRST GENTLEMAN   I'll do anything now that is virtuous,
  but I am out of the road of rutting forever.   *Exeunt.* 9

                         ✻

∾ **IV.6** *Enter [Pander, Bawd, and Boult].*

PANDER   Well, I had rather than twice the worth of her
  she had ne'er come here.
BAWD   Fie, fie upon her! she's able to freeze the god Pria-   3
  pus and undo a whole generation. We must either get   4

---

44 *visor* mask   47–48 *bear ... Fortune* allow his course to be directed by
Fortune   49 *well-a-day* grief
   IV.5 Mytilene: the brothel   9 *rutting* lechery
   IV.6 The brothel   3–4 *the god Priapus* the god of fertility, represented
with an erection   4 *undo ... generation* prevent a whole generation of chil-
dren from being conceived

her ravished or be rid of her. When she should do for
6   clients her fitment, and do me the kindness of our profession, she has me her quirks, her reasons, her master
reasons, her prayers, her knees, that she would make a
9   puritan of the devil if he should cheapen a kiss of her.
10   BOULT   Faith, I must ravish her, or she'll disfurnish us of
11   all our *cavalleria* and make our swearers priests.
12   PANDER   Now the pox upon her greensickness for me!
13   BAWD   Faith, there's no way to be rid on't but by the way
to the pox. Here comes the Lord Lysimachus disguised.
15   BOULT   We should have both lord and lown if the peevish
baggage would but give way to customers.
         Enter Lysimachus.
17   LYSIMACHUS   How now? How a dozen of virginities?
18   BAWD   Now the gods to-bless your honor.
     BOULT   I am glad to see your honor in good health.
20   LYSIMACHUS   You may so; 'tis the better for you that your
21   resorters stand upon sound legs. How now wholesome
22   iniquity have you that a man may deal withal and defy
the surgeon?
     BAWD   We have here one, sir, if she would – but there
never came her like in Mytilene.
26   LYSIMACHUS   If she'd do the deeds of darkness, thou
wouldst say.
28   BAWD   Your honor knows what 'tis to say well enough.
     LYSIMACHUS   Well, call forth, call forth.

---

6 *fitment* duty, what befits her as a prostitute   6–7 *do me, has me* do, has
(grammatically, ethical datives)   9 *cheapen* bargain for   11 *cavalleria* cava-
liers   12 *the pox* literally, syphilis (a generalized curse, but here particularly
appropriate); *greensickness* anemic condition of adolescent girls, thought to
result from a lack of sexual activity – hence, here, pathological virginity; *for
me* say I   13 *on't* of it   15 *lord and lown* lords and lower-class men; *peevish*
obstinate   17 *How a dozen* how much for a dozen   18 *to-bless* thoroughly
bless   21 *resorters* customers   21–22 *How . . . you* (either "what healthy
whore have you," or *wholesome iniquity* is an ironic address to the bawd)
22–23 *deal . . . surgeon* have sex with and not require a doctor   26 *the deeds
of darkness* sexual acts   28 *what . . . say* how to put it

BOULT   For flesh and blood, sir, white and red, you shall   30
see a rose; and she were a rose indeed, if she had but –   31
LYSIMACHUS   What, prithee?
BOULT   O, sir, I can be modest.
LYSIMACHUS   That dignifies the renown of a bawd, no less   34
than it gives a good report to a number to be chaste.   35
                                                [Exit Boult.]
BAWD   Here comes that which grows to the stalk – never   36
plucked yet, I can assure you.
     [Enter Boult with Marina.]
Is she not a fair creature?
LYSIMACHUS   Faith, she would serve after a long voyage   39
at sea. *[Paying the Bawd]* Well, there's for you. Leave us.   40
BAWD   I beseech your honor give me leave a word, and   41
I'll have done presently.
LYSIMACHUS   I beseech you do.
BAWD   *[To Marina]* First, I would have you note this is
an honorable man.
MARINA   I desire to find him so, that I may worthily note   46
him.
BAWD   Next, he's the governor of this country, and a man
whom I am bound to.   49
MARINA   If he govern the country, you are bound to him   50
indeed; but how honorable he is in that, I know not.
BAWD   Pray you, without any more virginal fencing, will   52
you use him kindly? He will line your apron with gold.
MARINA   What he will do graciously, I will thankfully re-   54
ceive.

---

31 *a rose . . . but* (the implied end of the sentence is "a prick": the proverb
says "there is no rose without a prick," and *rose* is a euphemism for vagina)
34 *That* modesty   35 *gives . . . chaste* gives a good many bawds a reputation
for chastity   36 *grows to* still grows on   39–40 *would . . . sea* would do for a
sex-starved sailor (Is Lysimachus unimpressed? Pretending to be unimpressed
to keep the price down? Dissembling how impressed he really is?)   41
give . . . word let me say a word to her   46 *worthily note* treat him with respect   49 *whom . . . bound to* (presumably for not closing her brothel down)
52 *virginal fencing* verbal fencing on behalf of virginity   54 *graciously* (1)
charitably, (2) like a gentleman

LYSIMACHUS Ha' you done?

57 BAWD My lord, she's not paced yet; you must take some
58 pains to work her to your manage. – Come, we will
leave his honor and her together. – Go thy ways.

[Exeunt Bawd, Pander, and Boult.]

60 LYSIMACHUS Now, pretty one, how long have you been
at this trade?

MARINA What trade, sir?

LYSIMACHUS Why, I cannot name't but I shall offend.

MARINA I cannot be offended with my trade. Please you
to name it.

LYSIMACHUS How long have you been of this profession?

MARINA E'er since I can remember.

68 LYSIMACHUS Did you go to't so young? Were you a
69 gamester at five, or at seven?

70 MARINA Earlier too, sir, if now I be one.

LYSIMACHUS Why, the house you dwell in proclaims you
72 to be a creature of sale.

MARINA Do you know this house to be a place of such
resort, and will come into't? I hear say you're of honor-
75 able parts, and are the governor of this place.

76 LYSIMACHUS Why, hath your principal made known
unto you who I am?

MARINA Who is my principal?

LYSIMACHUS Why, your herb woman, she that sets seeds
80 and roots of shame and iniquity. O, you have heard
something of my power, and so stand aloof for more se-
82 rious wooing. But I protest to thee, pretty one, my authority shall not see thee, or else look friendly upon
thee. Come, bring me to some private place. Come,
come!

---

57 *paced* broken in, trained 58 *manage* control (the imagery is from horse-
manship) 68 *go to't* have sex 69 *gamester* whore 72 *of sale* who sells herself 75 *parts* qualities 76 *principal* employer 82–84 *my . . . . upon thee*
i.e., in my position, I cannot woo you seriously

MARINA

  If you were born to honor, show it now;

  If put upon you, make the judgment good   87

  That thought you worthy of it.

LYSIMACHUS

  How's this? how's this? Some more; be sage.   89

MARINA   For me,

  That am a maid, though most ungentle fortune   *90*

  Have placed me in this sty, where, since I came,   91

  Diseases have been sold dearer than physic –   92

  That the gods

  Would set me free from this unhallowed place,

  Though they did change me to the meanest bird   95

  That flies i' th' purer air!

LYSIMACHUS   I did not think

  Thou couldst have spoke so well; ne'er dreamt thou

    couldst.

  Had I brought hither a corrupted mind,

  Thy speech had altered it. Hold, here's gold for thee.

  Persever in that clear way thou goest,   *100*

  And the gods strengthen thee.

MARINA   The good gods preserve you!

LYSIMACHUS

  For me, be you thoughten   102

  That I came with no ill intent; for to me

  The very doors and windows savor vilely.

  Fare thee well. Thou art a piece of virtue, and   105

  I doubt not but thy training hath been noble.

  Hold, here's more gold for thee.

  A curse upon him, die he like a thief,

  That robs thee of thy goodness! If thou dost

  Hear from me, it shall be for thy good.   *110*

---

87 *put . . . . you* honor was conferred upon you   89 *be sage* (most editors assume this is spoken sarcastically, but it depends how quickly one wishes Lysimachus's conversion to take place)   91 *sty* pigsty   92 *Diseases . . . physic* the clients have paid more for disease than for medicine   95 *meanest* humblest 102 *be . . . thoughten* think to yourself   105 *piece* masterpiece

[Enter Boult.]

111 BOULT   I beseech your honor, one piece for me.

LYSIMACHUS

112   Avaunt, thou damnèd doorkeeper!
Your house, but for this virgin that doth prop it,
Would sink, and overwhelm you. Away!   *[Exit.]*

BOULT   How's this? We must take another course with
116   you. If your peevish chastity, which is not worth a
117   breakfast in the cheapest country under the cope, shall
undo a whole household, let me be gelded like a
spaniel. Come your ways.

120 MARINA   Whither would you have me?

BOULT   I must have your maidenhead taken off, or the
122   common hangman shall execute it. Come your ways.
We'll have no more gentlemen driven away. Come your
ways, I say.

Enter Bawd.

BAWD   How now? What's the matter?

BOULT   Worse and worse, mistress. She has here spoken
holy words to the Lord Lysimachus.

BAWD   O abominable!

BOULT   She makes our profession as it were to stink afore
130   the face of the gods.

BAWD   Marry, hang her up forever!

BOULT   The nobleman would have dealt with her like a
nobleman, and she sent him away as cold as a snowball;
saying his prayers too.

BAWD   Boult, take her away; use her at thy pleasure.
Crack the glass of her virginity and make the rest mal-
leable.

138 BOULT   An if she were a thornier piece of ground than
she is, she shall be plowed.

140 MARINA   Hark, hark, you gods!

---

111 *piece* gold piece   112 *Avaunt* away   116 *peevish* obstinate   117 *cope*
sky   122 *hangman* executioner (who takes heads off)   138 *An if* even if

BAWD   She conjures. Away with her! Would she had   141
    never come within my doors! – Marry hang you! –
    She's born to undo us. – Will you not go the way of
    womenkind? Marry come up, my dish of chastity with   144
    rosemary and bays!   *[Exit.]*   145
BOULT   Come, mistress; come your ways with me.
MARINA   Whither wilt thou have me?
BOULT   To take from you the jewel you hold so dear.
MARINA   Prithee tell me one thing first.
BOULT   Come now, your one thing.   150
MARINA
    What canst thou wish thine enemy to be?   151
BOULT   Why, I could wish him to be my master, or
    rather my mistress.
MARINA
    Neither of these are so bad as thou art,
    Since they do better thee in their command.   155
    Thou hold'st a place for which the painèd'st fiend
    Of hell would not in reputation change.
    Thou art the damnèd doorkeeper to every
    Coistrel that comes inquiring for his Tib.   159
    To the choleric fisting of every rogue   160
    Thy ear is liable. Thy food is such
    As hath been belched on by infected lungs.
BOULT   What would you have me do? go to the wars,
    would you? where a man may serve seven years for the   164
    loss of a leg, and have not money enough in the end to
    buy him a wooden one?

---

141 *conjures* invokes supernatural aid   144 *Marry come up* "Get over it!"
145 *rosemary and bays* (the herbal garnish for the *dish;* cf. l. 79, *your herb woman*)   151 *What ... be* what's the worst thing you could wish on your enemy   155 *they ... command* they are better than you because they give you orders   159 *Coistrel* scoundrel; *Tib* (generic name for a cat, hence, whore)   160–61 *To ... liable* your ear is liable to be boxed by any angry rogue   164–65 *for ... leg* only to lose his leg

MARINA
    Do anything but this thou doest. Empty
168   Old receptacles, or common shores, of filth;
169   Serve by indenture to the common hangman.
170   Any of these ways are yet better than this;
    For what thou professest, a baboon, could he speak,
172   Would own a name too dear. That the gods
    Would safely deliver me from this place!
    Here, here's gold for thee.
    If that thy master would gain by me,
    Proclaim that I can sing, weave, sew, and dance,
177   With other virtues, which I'll keep from boast;
    And I will undertake all these to teach.
    I doubt not but this populous city will
180   Yield many scholars.
BOULT   But can you teach all this you speak of?
MARINA
182   Prove that I cannot, take me home again
183   And prostitute me to the basest groom
    That doth frequent your house.
BOULT   Well, I will see what I can do for thee. If I can
    place thee, I will.
MARINA   But amongst honest women.
BOULT   Faith, my acquaintance lies little amongst them.
    But since my master and mistress hath bought you,
190   there's no going but by their consent. Therefore I will
    make them acquainted with your purpose, and I doubt
    not but I shall find them tractable enough. Come, I'll
    do for thee what I can. Come your ways.   *Exeunt.*

*

---

168 *common shores* riverbanks or seashores (where garbage was left to be washed away by the tide) **169** *by indenture* as an apprentice **172** *Would . . . dear* would value his honor too highly (i.e., even a baboon wouldn't stoop to what you do) **177** *virtues* skills; *I'll keep . . . boast* I won't boast about **182** *Prove* if you find **183** *groom* stableboy

❧ **V.Cho.** *Enter Gower.*

GOWER
  Marina thus the brothel scapes and chances
    Into an honest house, our story says.
  She sings like one immortal, and she dances
    As goddesslike to her admirèd lays;   4
  Deep clerks she dumbs; and with her neele composes   5
    Nature's own shape of bud, bird, branch, or berry,
  That even her art sisters the natural roses;   7
    Her inkle, silk, twin with the rubied cherry;   8
  That pupils lacks she none of noble race,
    Who pour their bounty on her; and her gain   10
  She gives the cursèd bawd. Here we her place;
    And to her father turn our thoughts again.
  Where we left him on the sea, we there him lost;
    Where, driven before the winds, he is arrived
  Here where his daughter dwells; and on this coast
    Suppose him now at anchor. The city strived
  God Neptune's annual feast to keep; from whence
    Lysimachus our Tyrian ship espies,
  His banners sable, trimmed with rich expense,   19
    And to him in his barge with fervor hies.   20
  In your supposing once more put your sight;   21
    Of heavy Pericles think this his bark,   22
  Where what is done in action – more, if might –   23
    Shall be discovered. Please you sit and hark.   *Exit.* 24

*

V.Cho. **4** *lays* songs **5** *Deep . . . dumbs* she renders learned scholars dumb
with amazement (at her learning); *neele* needle **7** *That* so that; *sisters* equals
8 *inkle* linen thread **19** *His* its; *sable* black **20** *him* it **21** *supposing* imagination **22** *heavy* sorrowful; *bark* ship **23** *more, if might* more would be enacted on the stage if it were possible **24** *discovered* revealed

❧ **V.1** *Enter Helicanus; to him two Sailors [, one of Tyre, the other of Mytilene].*

FIRST SAILOR   *[To the Sailor of Mytilene]*
1   Where is Lord Helicanus? He can resolve you.
     O, here he is.
     Sir, there is a barge put off from Mytilene,
     And in it is Lysimachus the governor,
     Who craves to come aboard. What is your will?
HELICANUS
     That he have his. Call up some gentlemen.
FIRST SAILOR   Ho, gentlemen! my lord calls.
     Enter two or three Gentlemen.
FIRST GENTLEMAN   Doth your lordship call?
HELICANUS
9   Gentlemen, there is some of worth would come
     aboard.
10   I pray ye greet them fairly.
                    [Exeunt Gentlemen and the two Sailors.]
     *Enter Lysimachus [and Lords, with the Gentlemen
     and the two Sailors].*
FIRST SAILOR
11   Sir, this is the man that can, in aught you would,
     Resolve you.
LYSIMACHUS   Hail, reverend sir, the gods preserve you.
HELICANUS
     And you, to outlive the age I am,
     And die as I would do.
LYSIMACHUS   You wish me well.
16   Being on shore, honoring of Neptune's triumphs,
     Seeing this goodly vessel ride before us,

V.1 On board Pericles' ship off Mytilene (Note: As the textual notes indicate, the text of this scene is unusually muddled, and has required a great deal of editorial intervention to make sense. What relation the result bears to the original sense there is, of course, no way of knowing.)   **1** *resolve* answer   **9** *some of worth* some noble persons   **11–12** *in . . . you* answer whatever you ask   **16** *triumphs* festivities

I made to it, to know of whence you are.

HELICANUS
First, what is your place?   19

LYSIMACHUS   I am the governor
Of this place you lie before.   20

HELICANUS
Sir, our vessel is of Tyre, in it the king;
A man who for this three months hath not spoken
To anyone, nor taken sustenance
But to prorogue his grief.   24

LYSIMACHUS
Upon what ground is his distemperature?   25

HELICANUS
'Twould be too tedious to repeat;
But the main grief springs from the loss
Of a belovèd daughter and a wife.

LYSIMACHUS
May we not see him?

HELICANUS   You may;
But bootless is your sight. He will not speak   30
To any.

LYSIMACHUS   Yet let me obtain my wish.

HELICANUS
Behold him.
    [Draws the curtain and reveals Pericles.]
                This was a goodly person
Till the disaster that, one mortal night,   33
Drove him to this.

LYSIMACHUS
Sir king, all hail, the gods preserve you!
Hail, royal sir!

HELICANUS
It is in vain; he will not speak to you.

---

19 *place* position   24 *prorogue* prolong   25 *distemperature* emotional disorder   30 *bootless* useless   33 *one mortal night* (when Thaisa died)

LORD
    Sir, we have a maid in Mytilene, I durst wager
    Would win some words of him.
LYSIMACHUS   'Tis well bethought.
40   She, questionless, with her sweet harmony
41   And other chosen attractions, would allure,
42   And make a battery through his deafened parts,
43   Which now are midway stopped.
44   She is all happy as the fairest of all,
45   And, with her fellow maids, is now upon
    The leafy shelter that abuts against
    The island's side.
              [Gives an order to a Lord, who departs.]
HELICANUS
    Sure, all effectless; yet nothing we'll omit
49   That bears recovery's name. But since your kindness
50   We have stretched thus far, let us beseech you
    That for our gold we may provision have,
52   Wherein we are not destitute for want,
    But weary for the staleness.
LYSIMACHUS   O, sir, a courtesy
    Which if we should deny, the most just gods
55   For every graff would send a caterpillar,
56   And so inflict our province. Yet once more
    Let me entreat to know at large the cause
    Of your king's sorrow.
HELICANUS   Sit, sir; I will recount it to you –
    But see, I am prevented.
        [Enter Lord with Marina and a Companion.]
LYSIMACHUS
60   O here's the lady that I sent for.
    Welcome, fair one. Is't not a goodly presence?

---

41 *chosen* choice 42 *make ... parts* assault his deaf ears 43 *midway stopped* half closed 44 *happy* fortunate 45 *upon* within 49 *bears ... name* can be called a cure 52–53 *Wherein ... staleness* i.e., we are in need not from poverty but from weariness at the tedium of our situation 55 *graff* cultivated (literally, grafted) plant 56 *inflict* afflict

HELICANUS
    She's a gallant lady.
LYSIMACHUS
    She's such a one that, were I well assured
    Came of a gentle kind and noble stock,   64
    I'd wish no better choice, and think me rarely wed.
        [To Marina]
    Fair one, all goodness that consists in beauty,   66
    Expect even here, where is a kingly patient,   67
    If that thy prosperous and artificial feat   68
    Can draw him but to answer thee in aught,
    Thy sacred physic shall receive such pay   70
    As thy desires can wish.
MARINA   Sir, I will use
    My utmost skill in his recovery, provided
    That none but I and my companion maid
    Be suffered to come near him.
LYSIMACHUS   Come, let us leave her;
    And the gods make her prosperous!   75
        [They withdraw.]

                The song [by Marina].

LYSIMACHUS   *[Advances.]*
    Marked he your music?
MARINA   No, nor looked on us.
LYSIMACHUS
    See, she will speak to him.
        [Withdraws again.]
MARINA
    Hail, sir; my lord, lend ear.

---

64 *gentle kind, noble stock* aristocratic family 66 *all . . . beauty* i.e., you who
embody all the goodness that resides in beauty 67 *Expect* (the object of the
verb is the clause in l. 70, [that] *Thy sacred physic shall receive such pay . . .*)
68 *prosperous . . . feat* bountiful and skillful art 75 s.d. *The song* (no text is
provided for the song)

PERICLES   Hum, ha!
        [Pushes her away.]
MARINA

80   I am a maid, my lord, that ne'er before
        Invited eyes, but have been gazed on like a comet.
        She speaks, my lord, that, may be, hath endured
        A grief might equal yours, if both were justly weighed.
84   Though wayward fortune did malign my state,
        My derivation was from ancestors
        Who stood equivalent with mighty kings;
87   But time hath rooted out my parentage,
88   And to the world and awkward casualties
        Bound me in servitude. *[Aside]* I will desist;
90   But there is something glows upon my cheek,
        And whispers in mine ear "Go not till he speak."
PERICLES
        My fortunes – parentage – good parentage –
        To equal mine – Was it not thus? What say you?
MARINA
        I said, my lord, if you did know my parentage,
        You would not do me violence.
PERICLES   I do think so.
        Pray you turn your eyes upon me.
97   You are like something that – What countrywoman?
        Here of these shores?
MARINA   No, nor of any shores.
99   Yet I was mortally brought forth, and am
100   No other than I appear.
PERICLES
        I am great with woe, and shall deliver weeping.
        My dearest wife was like this maid, and such a one
103   My daughter might have been. My queen's square
            brows;

---

84 *wayward* capricious   **87** *rooted out* uprooted   **88** *awkward casualties*
painful accidents   **97** *What countrywoman* what is your nationality   **99**
mortally (1) humanly (i.e., I am not a spirit), (2) out of death   **103** *square
brows* broad forehead

Her stature to an inch; as wandlike straight;
As silver-voiced; her eyes as jewel-like,
And cased as richly; in pace another Juno;   106
Who starves the ears she feeds, and makes them hun-
     gry,
The more she gives them speech. Where do you live?
MARINA
Where I am but a stranger. From the deck
You may discern the place.   *110*
PERICLES   Where were you bred?
And how achieved you these endowments which
You make more rich to owe?   112
MARINA
If I should tell my history, it would seem
Like lies disdained in the reporting.   114
PERICLES   Prithee speak.
Falseness cannot come from thee, for thou lookest
Modest as justice, and thou seemest a palace
For the crowned truth to dwell in. I will believe thee,
And make my senses credit thy relation   118
To points that seem impossible; for thou lookest
Like one I loved indeed. What were thy friends?   120
Didst thou not say, when I did push thee back –
Which was when I perceived thee – that thou cam'st
From good descending?
MARINA   So indeed I did.
PERICLES
Report thy parentage. I think thou said'st
Thou hadst been tossed from wrong to injury,
And that thou thought'st thy griefs might equal mine,
If both were opened.   127
MARINA   Some such thing

---

106 *cased . . . richly* i.e., set in as beautiful a face; *pace* stride; *Juno* queen of
heaven, embodiment of majesty 112 *to owe* in possessing 114 *disdained . . . reporting* disowned as soon as they are told 118 *credit . . . relation* believe your story 120 *What . . . friends* who were your relations 127
opened revealed

I said, and said no more but what my thoughts
Did warrant me was likely.
PERICLES   Tell thy story.
130 If thine, considered, prove the thousandth part
131 Of my endurance, thou art a man, and I
     Have suffered like a girl. Yet thou dost look
133 Like Patience gazing on kings' graves and smiling
     Extremity out of act. What were thy friends?
     How lost thou them? Thy name, my most kind virgin?
     Recount, I do beseech thee. Come, sit by me.
MARINA
     My name is Marina.
PERICLES   O, I am mocked,
     And thou by some incensèd god sent hither
     To make the world to laugh at me.
MARINA   Patience, good sir,
140 Or here I'll cease.
PERICLES   Nay, I'll be patient.
     Thou little know'st how thou dost startle me
     To call thyself Marina.
MARINA
     The name was given me by one that had some power –
     My father, and a king.
PERICLES   How? a king's daughter?
     And called Marina?
MARINA   You said you would believe me;
     But, not to be a troubler of your peace,
     I will end here.
PERICLES   But are you flesh and blood?
     Have you a working pulse? and are no fairy?
149 No motion? Well, speak on. Where were you born?
150 And wherefore called Marina?
MARINA   Called Marina
     For I was born at sea.

---

131 *my endurance* what I have endured   133–34 *smiling . . . act* calmly facing down the most violent acts   149 *motion* puppet show

PERICLES   At sea? What mother?
MARINA
  My mother was the daughter of a king;
  Who died the very minute I was born,
  As my good nurse Lychorida hath oft
  Delivered weeping.   155
PERICLES   O, stop there a little!
  This is the rarest dream that e'er dulled sleep   156
  Did mock sad fools withal. This cannot be   157
  My daughter, buried. – Well, where were you bred?
  I'll hear you more, to th' bottom of your story,
  And never interrupt you.   160
MARINA   You scorn; believe me,
  'Twere best I did give o'er.
PERICLES
  I will believe you by the syllable   162
  Of what you shall deliver. Yet give me leave:
  How came you in these parts? Where were you bred?
MARINA
  The king my father did in Tarsus leave me,
  Till cruel Cleon, with his wicked wife,
  Did seek to murder me; and having wooed
  A villain to attempt it, who having drawn to do't,   168
  A crew of pirates came and rescued me;
  Brought me to Mytilene. But, good sir,   170
  Whither will you have me? Why do you weep? It may 171
    be,
  You think me an impostor. No, good faith,
  I am the daughter to King Pericles,
  If good King Pericles be.   174
PERICLES   Ho, Helicanus!
HELICANUS   Calls my lord?

---

155 *Delivered weeping* reported in tears 156 *dulled sleep* sleep that dulls us
157 *withal* with 162 *by* down to 168 *drawn* drawn his sword 171
Whither . . . me where are your questions leading me 174 *be* live

PERICLES
    Thou art a grave and noble counselor,
177   Most wise in general. Tell me, if thou canst,
178   What this maid is, or what is like to be,
    That thus hath made me weep?
HELICANUS   I know not; but
180   Here's the regent, sir, of Mytilene
    Speaks nobly of her.
LYSIMACHUS   She never would tell
    Her parentage. Being demanded that,
    She would sit still and weep.
PERICLES
    O Helicanus, strike me, honored sir,
    Give me a gash, put me to present pain,
    Lest this great sea of joys rushing upon me
    O'erbear the shores of my mortality
    And drown me with their sweetness. O, come hither,
    Thou that beget'st him that did thee beget;
190   Thou that wast born at sea, buried at Tarsus,
    And found at sea again – O Helicanus,
    Down on thy knees, thank the holy gods as loud
    As thunder threatens us. This is Marina.
        [Helicanus kneels.]
    What was thy mother's name? Tell me but that,
    For truth can never be confirmed enough,
196   Though doubts did ever sleep.
MARINA   First, sir, I pray,
    What is your title?
PERICLES
    I am Pericles of Tyre. But tell me now
    My drowned queen's name, as in the rest you said
200   Thou hast been godlike perfect.
    The heir of kingdoms, and another like
    To Pericles thy father.

---

177 *in general* in all things 178 *like* likely 196 *Though . . . sleep* even
though doubts are laid to rest

MARINA   *[Kneeling]*
   Is it no more to be your daughter than
   To say my mother's name was Thaisa?
   Thaisa was my mother, who did end
   The minute I began.
PERICLES
   Now blessing on thee: rise; thou art my child.
      [They rise.]
   Give me fresh garments. Mine own Helicanus,
   She is not dead at Tarsus, as she should have been,   209
   By savage Cleon. She shall tell thee all;   210
   When thou shalt kneel, and justify in knowledge   211
   She is thy very princess. – Who is this?
HELICANUS
   Sir, 'tis the Governor of Mytilene,
   Who, hearing of your melancholy state,
   Did come to see you.
PERICLES   I embrace you.
   Give me my robes. I am wild in my beholding.   216
   O heavens bless my girl! *[Music.]* But hark, what   217
      music?
   Tell Helicanus, my Marina, tell him
   O'er, point by point, for yet he seems to doubt,
   How sure you are my daughter. But what music?   220
HELICANUS
   My lord, I hear none.
PERICLES   None?
   The music of the spheres! List, my Marina.   222
LYSIMACHUS
   It is not good to cross him. Give him way.

---

209 *as . . . been* as she was intended to be   **211** *justify in knowledge* confirm
that   **216** *wild . . . beholding* (1) unkempt in appearance, (2) ecstatic as I
watch   **217 s.d.** *[Music.]* (only Pericles hears the celestial music, but the audience hears what he hears, as it sees the vision of Diana at l. 231)   **222**
music . . . spheres the celestial harmony produced, according to Ptolemaic as-
tronomy, by the motion of the planets and stars

PERICLES
    Rarest sounds. Do ye not hear?
LYSIMACHUS
    Music, my lord? I hear.
PERICLES   Most heavenly music,
226   It nips me unto listening, and thick slumber
    Hangs upon mine eyes. Let me rest.
    [Sleeps.]
LYSIMACHUS
    A pillow for his head. So, leave him all.
229   Well, my companion friends, if this but answer
230   To my just belief, I'll well remember you.
                           [Exeunt all but Pericles.]
    Diana [descends from the heavens].

DIANA
    My temple stands in Ephesus. Hie thee thither
        And do upon mine altar sacrifice.
    There, when my maiden priests are met together,
234   Before the people all
    Reveal how thou at sea didst lose thy wife.
236   To mourn thy crosses, with thy daughter's, call,
237   And give them repetition to the life.
238   Or perform my bidding, or thou livest in woe;
    Do't, and happy, by my silver bow.
240   Awake, and tell thy dream.   *[She ascends.]*
PERICLES
241   Celestial Dian, goddess argentine,
    I will obey thee. Helicanus!
    [Enter Helicanus, Lysimachus, and Marina.]
HELICANUS   Sir?
PERICLES
    My purpose was for Tarsus, there to strike

---

226 *nips . . . unto* draws me into 229–30 *if . . . belief* if this turns out as I anticipate 230 *remember* reward 234 *Before . . . all* (two more feet rhyming with *sacrifice* are clearly missing) 236 *crosses* sufferings 237 *give . . . life* recount them accurately 238 *Or* either 241 *argentine* silver (Diana's emblematic color, as the moon goddess)

The inhospitable Cleon; but I am
For other service first. Toward Ephesus
Turn our blown sails; eftsoons I'll tell thee why.   246
      [To Lysimachus]
Shall we refresh us, sir, upon your shore,
And give you gold for such provision
As our intents will need?

LYSIMACHUS
Sir, with all my heart; and, when you come ashore,   250
I have another suit.

PERICLES   You shall prevail,
Were it to woo my daughter; for it seems
You have been noble towards her.

LYSIMACHUS
Sir, lend me your arm.

PERICLES   Come, my Marina.   *Exeunt.*
                         *

∾ **V.2** *Enter Gower.*

GOWER
Now our sands are almost run;
More a little, and then dumb.
This, my last boon, give me,   3
For such kindness must relieve me: 4
That you aptly will suppose   5
What pageantry, what feats, what shows,
What minstrelsy and pretty din
The regent made in Mytilin
To greet the king. So he thrived   9
That he is promised to be wived   10
To fair Marina; but in no wise   11

---

246 *blown* full; *eftsoons* later
   V.2 3 *boon* favor **4** *relieve me* release me (from my responsibilities to
the story) **5** *aptly . . . suppose* will readily imagine **9** *he* Lysimachus **11**
wise way

12 Till he had done his sacrifice,
    As Dian bade; whereto being bound,
14 The interim, pray you, all confound.
15 In feathered briefness sails are filled,
    And wishes fall out as they're willed.
    At Ephesus the temple see,
    Our king, and all his company.
    That he can hither come so soon
20 Is by your fancies' thankful doom.   *[Exit.]*

                              *

∾ **V.3** *Enter Pericles, Lysimachus, Helicanus, Marina,*
    and others [at one door, Thaisa with other Vestals and
    Cerimon at the other].

PERICLES
    Hail, Dian. To perform thy just command,
    I here confess myself the King of Tyre;
    Who, frighted from my country, did wed
    At Pentapolis the fair Thaisa.
    At sea in childbed died she, but brought forth
    A maid child called Marina, who, O goddess,
7   Wears yet thy silver livery. She at Tarsus
    Was nursed with Cleon; who at fourteen years
    He sought to murder; but her better stars
10 Brought her to Mytilene; 'gainst whose shore
11 Riding, her fortunes brought the maid aboard us,
    Where, by her own most clear remembrance, she
13 Made known herself my daughter.
THAISA   Voice and favor –
    You are, you are – O royal Pericles!
        [She faints.]

_____

12 *he* Pericles; *done . . . sacrifice* performed his duty 14 *interim . . . con-*
found i.e., abolish the intervening time 15 *feathered briefness* winged speed
20 *your . . . doom* the gracious will of your imagination
    V.3 The temple of Diana at Ephesus 7 *Wears . . . . livery* i.e., is still your
virgin votary 11 *Riding* when we were at anchor 13 *favor* face

PERICLES
　What means the nun? She dies! Help, gentlemen!
CERIMON
　Noble sir,
　If you have told Diana's altar true,
　This is your wife.　　　　　　　　　　　　　　　　　18
PERICLES　　　　　　　　Reverend appearer, no.
　I threw her overboard with these very arms.
CERIMON
　Upon this coast, I warrant you.　　　　　　　　　20
PERICLES　　　　　　　　　　'Tis most certain.
CERIMON
　Look to the lady. O, she's but overjoyed.
　Early in blustering morn this lady was
　Thrown upon this shore. I oped the coffin,
　Found there rich jewels; recovered her, and placed her　24
　Here in Diana's temple.
PERICLES　　　　　　　　May we see them?
CERIMON
　Great sir, they shall be brought you to my house,
　Whither I invite you. Look, Thaisa is
　Recovered.
THAISA　　　　　O, let me look!
　If he be none of mine, my sanctity　　　　　　　29
　Will to my sense bend no licentious ear,　　　　30
　But curb it, spite of seeing. O my lord,
　Are you not Pericles? Like him you spake;
　Like him you are. Did you not name a tempest,
　A birth, and death?
PERICLES　　　　　　　The voice of dead Thaisa!
THAISA
　That Thaisa am I, supposèd dead
　And drowned.

---

18 *Reverend appearer* you who appear worthy of reverence　24 *recovered* revived　29–30 *If. . . ear* if he is not my husband, my holy state will not let me feel desire for him

PERICLES
   Immortal Dian!
THAISA   Now I know you better.
38   When we with tears parted Pentapolis,
   The king my father gave you such a ring.
     [Points to his ring.]
PERICLES
40   This, this! No more, you gods! your present kindness
41   Makes my past miseries sports. You shall do well
   That on the touching of her lips I may
   Melt and no more be seen. O, come, be buried
   A second time within these arms!
MARINA   My heart
   Leaps to be gone into my mother's bosom.
     [Kneels to Thaisa.]
PERICLES
   Look who kneels here. Flesh of thy flesh, Thaisa;
   Thy burden at the sea, and called Marina,
48   For she was yielded there.
THAISA   Blessed, and mine own!
HELICANUS
   Hail, madam, and my queen.
THAISA   I know you not.
PERICLES
50   You have heard me say, when I did fly from Tyre,
   I left behind an ancient substitute.
   Can you remember what I called the man?
   I have named him oft.
THAISA   'Twas Helicanus then.
PERICLES
   Still confirmation.
   Embrace him, dear Thaisa; this is he.
   Now do I long to hear how you were found;
   How possibly preserved; and who to thank,

---

38 *parted* departed from **41–43** *You . . . Melt* i.e., if I am utterly annihilated in her kiss, the gods will have done well **48** *yielded* born

Besides the gods, for this great miracle.

THAISA
Lord Cerimon, my lord; this man,
Through whom the gods have shown their power, that   60
  can
From first to last resolve you.   61

PERICLES   Reverend sir,
The gods can have no mortal officer
More like a god than you. Will you deliver   63
How this dead queen relives?

CERIMON   I will, my lord.
Beseech you first, go with me to my house,
Where shall be shown you all was found with her;
How she came placed here in the temple;
No needful thing omitted.

PERICLES   Pure Dian,
Bless thee for thy vision; and will offer   69
Night oblations to thee. Thaisa,   70
This prince, the fair betrothèd of your daughter,
Shall marry her at Pentapolis;
And now this ornament makes me look dismal   73
Will I clip to form,   74
And what this fourteen years no razor touched,
To grace thy marriage day I'll beautify.

THAISA
Lord Cerimon hath letters of good credit, sir,   77
My father's dead.

PERICLES
Heavens make a star of him. Yet there, my queen,   79
We'll celebrate their nuptials, and ourselves   80
Will in that kingdom spend our following days.
Our son and daughter shall in Tyrus reign.

---

61 *resolve you* satisfy you   63 *deliver* explain   69 *will* I will   70 *Night oblations* nightly prayers   73 *this ornament* (his uncut hair); *makes* that makes
74 *to form* into shape   77 *letters . . . credit* trustworthy letters   79 *there* (in
Pentapolis)

83   Lord Cerimon, we do our longing stay
      To hear the rest untold. Sir, lead's the way.   *[Exeunt.]*

                            *

∾ **Epi.**   [EPILOGUE
                spoken by] *Gower.*

      In Antiochus and his daughter you have heard
      Of monstrous lust the due and just reward;
      In Pericles, his queen, and daughter, seen,
      Although assailed with fortune fierce and keen,
5   Virtue preserved from fell destruction's blast,
      Led on by heaven, and crowned with joy at last.
      In Helicanus may you well descry
      A figure of truth, of faith, of loyalty.
      In reverend Cerimon there well appears
10   The worth that learnèd charity aye wears.
11   For wicked Cleon and his wife, when fame
      Had spread their cursèd deed to th' honored name
13   Of Pericles, to rage the city turn,
14   That him and his they in his palace burn.
      The gods for murder seemèd so content
      To punish, although not done, but meant.
      So, on your patience evermore attending,
      New joy wait on you. Here our play has ending.

                                        [Exit.]

---

83 *our . . . stay* put off our desire
   Epi. 5 *fell* cruel   10 *aye* always   11 *fame* rumor   13 *turn* (plural because *city* is being treated as a collective noun – cf. *they* in the next line)   14 *That* so that

AVAILABLE FROM PENGUIN CLASSICS

THE PELICAN SHAKESPEARE

The Comedy of Errors • Coriolanus • Henry VI, Part 1

Henry VIII • Love's Labor's Lost • The Two Gentlemen of Verona

General Editors: Stephen Orgel and A. R. Braunmuller
New Illustrated Covers designed by Manuja Waldia

AVAILABLE FROM PENGUIN CLASSICS

THE PELICAN SHAKESPEARE

Antony and Cleopatra • Henry IV, Part 2 • Measure for Measure

The Sonnets • Troilus and Cressida • The Winter's Tale

General Editors: Stephen Orgel and A. R. Braunmuller

New Illustrated Covers designed by Manuja Waldia